Forging the Iron Mind

by
Steven Mager

Copyright © 2018 by Steven Mager
ISBN-13: 978-0-692-12949-4

All rights reserved.

No part of this book may be reproduced in any form or by any electronic or mechanical means, including information storage and retrieval systems, without written permission from the author, except for the use of brief quotations in a book review.

• This book is not intended as a substitute for the medical advice of physicians. The reader should regularly consult a physician in matters relating to his/her health and particularly with respect to any symptoms that may require diagnosis or medical attention.

To my mother and my late father, who were made of iron before I knew what that meant.

Contents

Section One - Iron Origins

Chapter I - What is the Iron Mind? - 12

Chapter II - My Story - 19

Chapter III - The Lenses of Life - 27

Chapter IV - Questioning the Experts - 35

Chapter V - Depression and Culture - 39

Chapter VI - Upgrade Your Mind - 44

Chapter VII - Music: The Ultimate Weapon - 48

Chapter VIII - The Toxicity Audit - 58

Chapter IX - A Systemic Overhaul - 69

Chapter X - Become What You Are - 73

Section Two - Iron Tactics

Chapter XI - Self-Talk - 82

Chapter XII - Affirmations - 85

Chapter XIII - Projection and Visualization - 89

Chapter XIV - Inventing an Enemy or Inspiration - 93

Chapter XV - Dominating the Frame Game - 98

Chapter XVI - The Power of Shame - 102

Chapter XVII - Shaping Your Reality - 105

Chapter XVIII - The Story of Future You - 111

Chapter XIX - Iron Attitude - 115

Chapter XX - The Humility Fetish - 127

Chapter XXI - The Spheres of Influence - 130

Chapter XXII - Playing To Win - 134

Chapter XXIII - Winning Mentality - 142

Chapter XXIV - Learn to Play the Game - 147

Chapter XXV - The Pence Process - 153

Chapter XXVI - Become the Machine - 158

Chapter XXVII - The War on Cigarettes - 166

Chapter XXVIII - Annihilate Stress - 169

Chapter XXIX - The Overrated List - 174

Section Three: The Iron Life

Chapter XXX - Serenity Through Order - 184

Chapter XXXI - The Media Addiction Vortex - 188

Chapter XXXII - Monetize Your Life - 194

Chapter XXXIII - Immunity of the Gods - 199

Chapter XXXIV - The Fairness Doctrine - 205

Chapter XXXV - Drama-Free Dating - 211

Chapter XXXVI - The Iron Lungs - 220

Chapter XXXVII - The Iron Body - 223

Chapter XXXVIII - The Iron Diet - 234

Chapter XXXIX - The Magic of Massage - 243

Chapter XL - Supplements: A Cautionary Tale - 246

Chapter XLI - Books are Power - 249

Chapter XLII - The Time Spiral - 252

Appendix A: The Iron Bands

1. Pantera - 260
2. Danzig - 262
3. Sabaton - 263
4. Powerwolf - 264
5. Agalloch - 266
6. Slayer - 267
7. Nile - 269

Appendix B: The Playlists

1. Steve's Ultimate Metal Playlist - 274
2. AJ's Ultimate Hip-Hop Playlist - 276

"The first and best of victories is for a man to conquer himself; to be conquered by himself is, of all things, the most shameful and vile."

-Plato, Plato's Laws, Book 1

SECTION ONE: IRON ORIGINS

Section One:

Iron Origins

If you are reading this book, chances are you are someone that wants to make massive changes in their life. Possibly you just want to be a little bit better than you are now. Perhaps you're an alcoholic and want to quit, or a second-tier competitor who is looking to break into the upper echelon of competition. It could be that you're overweight and want to get into shape. If any of that or something else regarding self-improvement is accurate, then I can assure you you'll find something of interest for you in this book.

I thought I'd write this chapter to prepare you and give a few tips. First of all let's get out of the way what this book is, and what it isn't. I am going to deliver a sledgehammer to your head at times, as I'm not into playing around. You will not need to decipher any esoteric nonsense, if there's one thing I can't stand, it's someone who can talk for days and not deliver one actionable piece of information. So I'm going to do my damnedest to stay on point. Furthermore, this isn't your college biology textbook. I'll keep the science jargon to a minimum and source things out in the footnotes for you.

I'm 40 years old. I've read a lot of "self-help" books, sat through many seminars, and developed my own approaches to life. I've never been satisfied with any of the "programs" or "systems" to improve one's life. I take nuggets from each book or seminar, but I've found all of them wholly lacking. Each one that I consume I notice is lacking in some significant way. Maybe it doesn't take enough about diet into account, or possibly the workout section is underrepresented, or it could be that it doesn't address the overall perception in the way one might see the world, or maybe it spends too much time on science, and not enough on action.

"Self-help" books typically fall into one of three categories:
1. Spiritual: Religious, Zen, Divine Source, Voodoo, Secrets, etc.
2. Science: Diet, Workout, Theory, or Thesis based.
3. Perception/Mental Tricks: Understanding the world around you and influencing it.

My concept of the Iron Mind is a fusion of them all into one cohesive framework and adds a few unexpected twists. I take any idea from any discipline necessary to achieve my ends. Thus you will find science, perception, mental trickery, and even some spirituality in the forthcoming pages.

Let's take a look at how this book is laid out and how to get the most from it. I have laid this book out very specifically to take you on a journey. In case you didn't notice from the Table of Contents, there's a hell of a lot of chapters. I want to distill the elements I'm trying to get across to their most pure and focused, designed to be read in the order presented. I have broken the book into three sections:
1. Iron Origins: This is where we lay the foundation and get your mind to a place where it's ready to get cocked, locked, and ready to rock. We have a lot of perceptions to shift and premises to destroy and reset before we can honestly start making significant changes.

2. Iron Tactics: This section is built on actual mental techniques and changing how you view both yourself and the world, as well as increasing the level of control you have over your state of mind.
3. Iron Life: We now step into the real world. This is the section that puts into practice all that we've learned in the preceding chapters. Everything you do in life that will apply these principles and changes.

That's it. You'll find I'm not a wordy guy; I like to get to the point and drive it home with a sledgehammer, so now that you're ready,

It's time to Forge the Iron Mind.

Chapter I

What is the Iron Mind?

I love the word Iron. It's short, concise, evokes power, durability, and it just sounds tough. When I decided to write a book on mental self-improvement, I knew I had to work the word Iron into the title somewhere. The dictionary, in addition to the actual metal, calls it "great strength, hardness, or determination." So with all that being said, what does it mean to Forge the Iron Mind? Forging The Iron Mind means you have the knowledge that you own, and can control your frame of mind, and can use it to push yourself to greater heights physically, emotionally, and mentally. Having the Iron Mind means you can be smarter, stronger, healthier, more stable, and live a more positive life. I didn't always believe this was possible. I didn't always believe that I could learn how to control my mind. I believe it now, and you will as well by the time I'm done.

Think of the different things required to achieve what you want in life. What skills will be necessary? What sacrifices need to be made? Think of all the attributes that you want to have. Confidence, strength, determination, ambition, empathy, kindness. The Iron Mind encompasses all of these attributes and more. One cannot erect a house with just one type of material. Think of the tools I'm going to give you as building your mind. Each technique, a piece to put toward the grand goal of changing or improving your life. No one thing will create the Iron Mind. It's a set of principles and techniques put into practice that builds the mind into a formidable weapon.

With that said, I'm about to tell you something very controversial. Something that flies in the face of virtually all of the modern orthodoxy and everything you know regarding mental health management. Henry Ford said "Whether you think you can or think you can't—you're right," and he was 100% correct, and I'm going to tell you why:

You control your Mind, not the other way around.

I know what some of you are thinking. That's impossible. Our thought processes are controlled by chemicals and neurons in our brains that we can't possibly influence. Things like depression are purely chemical based problems, and medical technology can help. We are taught these days that nothing is our fault. Being depressed, being fat, or unhappy are just things that happen to us. I'm here to tell you a hard truth: It is almost entirely your fault. Not necessarily the things that happened to you, but how you handled them. Fortunately, I'm here to guide you to the light, and true happiness and control over your own life. You are not helpless in controlling your mind. Now, I assume some of you acknowledge that you have some degree of control over your mind frame, but just want to take it to the next level. That's great as well, but I believe most people don't understand the degree to which they control their mind.

Now, I'm about to revolutionize your life. To an astonishing degree, your mind is under your control. Think of it like this: Imagine your body is a computer. The internal organs are the various parts of a computer. A computer is of no use whatsoever without software. You must think of your mind as the operating system for your body. Now, realize this: An operating system can be programmed. It can have new skills (programs) installed onto it. It can be hacked and changed to suit the users' needs. Your mind is the operating system for the body. Once you understand this, and you understand that you can take control of your mind just as you would a computer, and shape how it thinks and thus how you feel, it is a very potent feeling. The human mind is remarkably powerful. It can be convinced, to the death, of aliens, gods, and the supernatural. It can be convinced that an alien lives in a volcano, on a planet hundreds of thousands of miles away. What did I just describe? Scientology, which a lot of people believe with every fiber of their being, and would die for in a second. The Norse believed wholeheartedly that the world was held up on a tree, Yggdrasil. This is a learned behavior, to absorb information, interpret it to suit our needs, and follow it to the death. The human "will to power" as Nietzsche called it, is capable of elevating to incredible levels or to be a slave to ideas. What I will teach you here, is to unlock the power of your mind. You can *decide* to take control of your mind, and I'm going to show you how.

First, you have to understand; your mind is your own. Up to this point, you've likely believed that a significant degree of your mind frame is not under your control. What I'm going to show you, is that not only is it under your control, but how to manipulate, or hack, your mind to make you better, happier, and more fulfilled. I will show you techniques you can use, in real life, to trick into, and eventually make real your Iron Mind. Some people try to use these tricks to convince themselves of something they know isn't true. That will not work. If you are overweight and low energy, no amount of convincing or trickery will eliminate the knowledge, deep down, that you are. You have to strive to make true the things that will benefit you. I watch things like the modern "body positive movement" and shake my head. These are individuals trying to convince themselves that being overweight and unhealthy is just fine. That being 400 pounds carries with it no consequence to their health. That will never work. For these "mind hacks" to work, you need to be hacking it into something you know is beneficial. I've met a lot of people in this movement, and they are never truly content. They try to pretend, but they always know deep down that they aren't, and resort to medication to try to make an untruth the reality. Moreover, they try to reshape society itself to conform to their version of reality, which will never result in true happiness.

The human body and mind are inextricably linked. A poisoned mind will degrade the body. A degraded body will poison the mind as well. There's significant evidence that one affects the other. This is why focusing on both is required to be the best you can be. You can try all the mind games you want, but if you have degraded your body, the mind will likely follow. Likewise, you can do all of the physical training you want, but if surrounded by toxic relationships that affect the mind, your fitness will eventually decline. Just as the computer cannot function without software, it cannot operate without a central processing unit. This is why it's vitally important to address both, and I have dedicated portions of this book for both.

>"You cannot carry a perfect soul in a cadaver of a body."

>-Friedrich Nietzsche

I will refer to Nietzsche often, as his work has had a profound impact on me. I believe any discussion of the power of the mind must include his work. Later, we explore some of his theories and others in the philosophy community as well. We read motivational quotes all the time, but just let them sail past us without really evaluating it or who said it. Take a look at the people who gave us those quotes. They had the Iron Mind. How did they get it? What tactics did they use? Some of these people may not even have a better IQ than you do, but they've learned how to harness their mind and use an indomitable will to shape their reality, and that of those around them. We will discuss some of these people in a later chapter, and how their techniques can elevate you as well. Those quotes exist for a reason; now it's time to learn from them and even make your own.

The other significant advantage of realizing that your mind is under your control is that once you believe it, a lot of positive elements become a self-fulfilling prophecy. Beneficial things become effortless to implement, and your will hardens because you know you are in control. Also, it becomes straightforward to flip the switch if the negative begins to creep into your mind. You become able to actively change your mood and mind frame, in a very small portion of time. I used to allow my bad moods to dominate my day. I'd go to work, and within 5 minutes something annoying would happen, and I'd shift into a bad mood for the rest of the day. In addition, I'd dwell on that one event, poisoning every interaction I'd have for the rest of the day. Once I learned how to change my own mind, I became able in seconds, to flip the entire episode into something positive so as not to ruin my day. Keep in mind this affects everyone with whom you interact. If you get into a bad mood and can't control it, it poisons everyone around you and becomes replicating.

Remember that you can't have a mind transplant (yet). You can't stick a USB or WIFI antenna in your brain to alter your mood. We aren't in the Matrix where you can download the ability to fly a helicopter in five seconds. The mind you have is the one you are stuck with for life. You have to master the one you have. We all have different genetics and characteristics. Some people are born savants, but most of us have to work hard to learn or achieve anything. Dwelling on the qualities you are born with helps nothing. You must realize that there are certain things you cannot influence in both life and body. The trick is to gain control of the things you CAN control, and your mind frame is absolutely one of them. You may not be able to stop your initial reaction to something, but you can change how you respond to that thing immediately thereafter. A prime example of this is Ray Lewis. Ray was extremely short and small for a middle linebacker. His physical characteristics alone would have wiped him off the list for most NFL teams. Ray, however, brought such a dominating mind frame, and unstoppable work ethic to the field that he ended up being one of the greatest defensive players to ever play the game. He had problems in his life at an early age, but he overcame them and became not only a dominating force on the field but a force for good as well. Your mind can overcome significant disadvantages, but it's up to you to make it happen. No one else can do it for you.

Now that you understand a fraction of the power of your mind, let's see how we can use this to our advantage. I ask you to read this book and make the changes listed. More than that though, I'm asking for something else:

I am asking you to believe.

I am asking you to believe that you can. I'm asking you to believe you can change your own mind for the better. If you believe it strongly enough, you can through sheer force, will yourself to believe it and become a better version of yourself. Ford, Ghandi, Jordan, they all believed it. These are not mythical gods, but real people that harnessed the power of the mind. They believed that the power of the mind created their reality, and that they were in control. Believe in yourself strongly enough, and you can quite literally will yourself to be a better person. You can change your own mind, and now that you know it can be done,

Let's get ready.

Chapter II

My Story

Dear Reader: I will tell you an incontrovertible fact. You can change your life. I know this because I have changed mine and have seen countless others do the same. I know some reading this are enduring problems I can't possibly understand, or know. What I can tell you is that I can help. Through my own experience, I will help you to harness the power within, the power that resides in the human mind. The human mind is capable of inventing and distorting reality, making you happy or sad, understand or reject truths, or produce an indomitable or fragile will.

I didn't always have the Iron Mind. Sometimes I fight to preserve it.

As I sit here, I've taken on the biggest challenge of my life. I quit a very comfortable job, to take a massive risk and put everything I have on the line. It's possible for me to lose everything I have in life. Yet, I don't worry. My will and determination will not allow for failure. This feeling of power, strength, and confidence most certainly did not come naturally, it had to be built. I will do my best to give you the tools necessary to change or improve your life.

I grew up in a split household. My parents divorced before my memory even begins. I stayed with my Mom most of the year, then went to my Dad's house for the Summer. I was an extremely reclusive child. I was the type of kid that wanted more than anything just to read or play video games. I hated any work or school. All I wanted to do was lay in front of either the TV or a book. Getting me out to mow the lawn or do any chores elicited whining, or finding excuses not to do it. I was also extremely doughy physically. I had very little muscle, as I tried to get as little actual work in as possible. I had very few friends as well. I invented imaginary friends and pictured myself in recreations of stories I'd read. I would even talk aloud to them when I didn't think people were looking.

My parents were amazing. Despite being divorced, they both contributed a significant part to my development. My mom was superhuman, managing a son, school, and work simultaneously. She worked her way up the ladder from an accountant to COO of her company. My Dad passed away recently, but I never will forget the ferocious work ethic, unbelievably vast skill set, and the dominating, confident personality he was. My parents, in different ways, are both my heroes. Despite their best efforts, neither could draw me out of my cloud of apathy. My Dad was always trying to teach me a new skill, and my Mom worked as hard as possible to give me every opportunity she could.

I got made fun of at school a lot. I went to a private Christian school, with a tiny group of students. I was tall for my school, but I was awful at sports. My lack of discipline, fitness, and coordination meant that I'd have a rough time. I got cut from the basketball team and got made fun of as the only six-footer not to make the team. Even in my senior year, I rode the bench the majority of the time. I don't remember what caused it, maybe I've blocked it out, but I was reduced to tears in front of a lot of people once. I was then bestowed with the nickname "Emotional" by some of the older kids. I was relentlessly mocked and given crying gestures on a regular basis. Wedgies were liberally given out as well. I had no confidence or belief in myself, and the bullies ate me up. Ironically, more than twenty years after, I see that bullying as a significant building block that I believe actually helped me in the long run.

I was also a huge nerd. Nowadays practically everyone is, but in the 80s and early 90s in a small school, virtually no one was. I had no outlet to talk to anyone about things I liked. For them, sports, girls, and mischief were the primary topics of discussion. I longed to have someone to talk with about games, books or other miscellaneous nerdy things. I tried virtually everything at school, from band class to sports, to fundraising, and none of it captured me. No class captured my attention, except History. To this day I still love History of all kinds. I failed Algebra and a year of Spanish. I barely made it through, academically. I always hated school, and would eventually drop out of my first semester at college. In addition, I was awful with girls. I had crushes, but zero confidence in talking to them. I always tried to play the nice guy, and be friends, which worked a grand total of zero times. I watched in jealousy as my friends dated girls I had crushes on. I was 17 when I had my first kiss, and I was out of high school for my first sexual experience. This produced over time an irrational hatred for women in my early 20s, and I actively went out of my way to be rude to them, even ones that showed interest. Therefore, I had few friends, and no girlfriend, so I retreated into myself. Inventing stories, talking to myself, playing games, and the like.

My first job was at Chic-Fil-A, in a mall, of which I really can't complain. For a first job, I can't imagine much better. A couple of customers were guys that worked at the local Electronics Boutique (now known as Gamestop). They were significantly older than I was, and I took every opportunity to go over and hang out with them in the store. All of them were funny, confident, and cool, the antithesis of what I was. However, we all loved games, and it was my goal to work there. To me, this was the dream job, to be able to talk about video games all day. Finally, one of that happiest days of my life up to that point happened: I was hired at Electronics Boutique. For a while, it was a blast. Talking about video games all day and getting paid for it was amazing. I thought my coworkers were the coolest guys alive. They were gamers, got girls, and generally had great fun. I started hanging out with them outside of work, and played lots of games, went to strip clubs, and had a great time. Until I was sold out.

There was a lot of inventory in the store missing. The manager convinced me that I was being blamed for it because I was the newest. He assured me that the District Manager was coming up to the store to fire and have me arrested. I was in such awe of my new friends, and so unwilling to stand up for myself that I ran away and never came back. The manager was so persuasive that I believed he was on my side, and would never sell me out. Come to find out, years later, he admitted to sacrificing me to his boss to keep his job. This was a constant theme of my life for a very long time, trusting, and getting stabbed in the back. However, the man that sold me out gave me the two of the most significant gifts in my life. The first was that he got me to work out. I hated myself. Every time I looked in the mirror, I averted my gaze. I felt and looked terrible. He decided to start working out, and given how much I idolized him, I was going to do whatever he did. The second was Heavy Metal music. It turned out to be one of the most positive things in my life and contributed one of the most significant parts of my Iron Mind. In this book, I'll look at how I used music to power myself, and how you can do the same regardless of genre. Periodically, I'll highlight an artist that has played a significant role in my development.

I remember my defining moment on the path to the Iron Mind. I remember I was sad, depressed, in debt, and drastically overweight. I routinely avoided mirrors whenever possible, because I didn't like what I saw. I wasn't confident, didn't have an ounce of muscle, and looked as though I was crafted from Pillsbury dough. I remember one day in my small apartment, where I caught a glimpse of myself shirtless in front of the mirror. I hated what I saw, but more than that I just felt terrible. I caught the glance of my eye in the mirror, and it was as if the entirety of my life flashed before my eyes, as though I were dying. It was a life I wasn't in any way happy with, that I hated. I remember staring at myself in the eyes and saying:

"No more."

Over the course of two decades, I transformed myself. I learned everything I could about working out and dieting and turned all my effort into becoming a force of nature. As my body hardened, so too did my mind. Early on, I still fundamentally lacked all of the mental techniques and control, but I forged forward with dogged determination. I got to the point where thought I was too tough to stop. My will was iron, and I just knew I would be fine to keep pushing forward. The work ethic my parents instilled was unstoppable. I thought aching elbows were no big deal, and I could tough it out. I was wrong. I didn't have enough mental mastery to know when to take a break, and I eventually had to have both elbow tendons reattached. Over the course of years of diagnosing, and finally surgery and rehab, I had to watch everything I built erode. The muscle I killed myself to get started to atrophy. I was so weak I could barely pick up anything, and I found myself sinking into depths of depression. The years of blood, sweat, and tears building myself all going down the drain. I became miserable to everyone, and I was borderline impossible to be around. It amazes me to this day that I never got fired. I took out my fury and depression on everyone around me.

I always used the gym and weightlifting to center myself and provide an outlet for my aggression. Without it, I was a terror. I was working in customer service at the time, and I managed to get into a confrontation on a near-daily basis. If not for the intervention of a boss I respected, I'm not sure how things would have ended. In addition, I had to come to a harsh truth: My powerlifting days were likely over. Up to that point, I still believed I could be what I once was, again. My self-worth was defined at the time by how much, and how hard, I could lift. Now, I reflect on that breakdown, and it was the best thing that could have happened. I still lift weights and stay active and healthy, but I do it for fun, and to stay in shape. My self-worth is no longer determined by how much I can lift. I take pride in the fact that I'm older now, and still in better shape than most 20-year-olds. I used to think assholes surrounded me, and I was the only one that "got it." Newsflash: If everyone around you is an asshole, maybe it isn't those people that are the problem. I blamed everyone around me continually for everything. I used to think everyone was working against me to ensure my failure. I eventually took ownership of my problems and broke down in tears in front of someone I had previously hated. They weren't the problem: I was. That realization was cathartic and allowed me to move on.

Ah, if only I could talk to my younger self! We all say that, and I couldn't disagree more. I used to think that occasionally. Now I realize that everything that's happened in my life has shaped me into the person I've become, one that I like. I have no regrets. Even the negative things that happened in my life, the girl I lost, the injuries I sustained, the bullies that got to me, have all shaped the man I've become. We need negative things to happen to us. It's how we are forged and build character. I look back on all the negatives, and how I've adapted and improved. How can one never experience adversity, and become better? I believe it to be impossible. We *need* adversity to shape us into our future selves. This is why the modern idea of safe spaces and trigger warnings are so dangerous. They keep us from confronting realities and overcoming challenges. In addition, I believe this contributes overwhelmingly to the suicide rates. We collectively as a society don't teach our kids how to handle adversity since everything is someone else fault, or out of our control.

You have to come to that "No More" point. You have to arrive at the point of DECIDING that your life is unacceptable. This is why just going on a diet to fix your weight isn't enough. It needs a full scale 24/7 assault on your mind frame and your entire life. I am going to do everything I can to put the tools I and others have used in your hands to make the consequential changes in your life possible. But first, you have to decide that this isn't just about losing weight, or gaining some muscle, or being a better person. Those are too small. You need to construct yourself out of Iron and build an entirely new person from the ground up who has a totally different view of the nature of reality. Once you change how you see the world, and how humans operate and get your shit together, then you can make changes that will endure. I'm not here to help you lose 5, 50, or 500 pounds. I'm here to help you change your life, permanently.

That's enough about me for now.

It's time to change your entire view of the world.

Chapter III

The Lenses of Life

I've got a lot planned for the upcoming chapters to help you change the game of life. First, though, I'm going to ask you to change your mental frame on things. We can't make changes if we don't examine everything we think we know about the mind. We can't start with just one element, such as "I want to lose weight, how do I do it," we have to start from the beginning before we even get to that part of the equation. A lot of people start in the wrong place, thus leading them to failure. If you start with the wrong frame on the world, then virtually every conclusion you come to after that is going to be suspect. This is why we need to rebuild from ground zero. We have to take the most fundamental starting point, and reexamine it and work down from there.

Let's take a look at how we all view the world. We all have a worldview, biases, and beliefs that we use to construct our vision of the world. Scott Adams of Dilbert fame calls this the "two movies on one screen" theory. We have all been in the situation where we watched the same movie with another person and saw two completely different things. You may have walked out convinced you saw the greatest movie of all time, and the person you went with hated it. I experienced this very thing upon viewing the new Star Wars movie The Last Jedi with a friend. Coming out of the theater, I was exhilarated. I loved every minute of it, and I was sure it was the best Star Wars movie since The Empire Strikes Back. I turned to my friend, and I swear he said: "God that was the worst Star Wars movie ever."

We saw the same thing. We sat side by side and saw the exact same event. We see this virtually every day with President Donald Trump. Half of America watches a Trump speech, convinced that they saw the next Hitler in action, and the other half sees the next savior of America.

Same speech.

Same movie.

What's different is the lens through which we see these things. I bring this up extremely early in this book because it is imperative that we change the lens through which you see the world. Think of your lens as a pair of glasses with multiple panes. Each pane is a different worldview or bias that shapes the event the glasses are showing you. You filter every single thing you experience in life through these lenses. Let me give you an example of how each lens works with the one before it to create an opinion on a topic. For this example, I will use The Last Jedi, the most recent Star Wars movie that generated an incredible amount of controversy, so there will be massive spoilers incoming.

Lens 1: I consider myself an honorable, virtuous person.

Lens 2: I always root for the hero to conquer evil.

Lens 3: As a child, I loved Star Wars.

Lens 4: Luke Skywalker conquered evil and became a legend.

Lens 5: I waited 16 years for a new Star Wars movie.

Lens 6: I expect Luke Skywalker to return and be the hero with which I grew up.

These are the lenses through which a lot of Star Wars fans saw the new movie. The movie they saw was a travesty of epic scale. Their childhood hero, Luke Skywalker, is a monumental failure in The Last Jedi, which shatters five of the six lenses in a row. They went into the movie expecting to see certain things, all influenced by their childhood, how they grew up, the toys they had, and how the previous films ended. If you look at most of the criticism of The Last Jedi, the vast majority centers around the portrayal of Luke. It bothered people a great deal that Luke turned out not to be the hero they had built up from the previous movies, and a lot of them had their entire viewpoint shattered by the Last Jedi. I bring this up because how you see the world is beyond critical to the development of the Iron Mind. Most people start with a goal such "I want to lose X amount of weight" and start from there.

What I want to do is deconstruct the lenses that you see the world through, thus making all of your lenses much easier to see through, and empowering you to understand how they work, and consequently reshaping your entire perception of reality. Let's take a hypothetical look at the lenses through which one might view the world currently.

Lens 1: I am a human, and I have a Mind.

Lens 2: I am a rational person.

Lens 3: I believe in science.

Lens 4: Science tells me I have depression.

Lens 5: I am taking anti-depressants.

Lens 6: I don't feel particularly great about myself, and I can't help it.

Lens 7: I'm not satisfied with the state of my marriage.

Lens 8: I know I need to make changes in my life.

Lens 9: I think losing weight might make me happier.

Lens 10: I need to lose 30 pounds.

If we start right now at lens 9, we are going to have problems, because we haven't addressed the earlier lenses. Before we get to lenses 9 and 10, we have to go wayyyyyyy back to lens TWO. That's right, all the way back to the beginning.

Understand this: You aren't rational. You just think you are.

Every study now shows that we all have implicit biases, and that we make almost every decision based on emotional content[1], that we then rationalize later[2]. Then we have lens three. As I'll show in the next chapters, science isn't foolproof and makes a lot of mistakes. That's the entire heart of the scientific method. Knowing this, we now have to question 3-5. Then, we have 6-8. These must be addressed before we

---

[1] https://perception.org/research/implicit-bias/
[2] https://www.psychologytoday.com/us/blog/theory-knowledge/201202/understanding-how-we-filter-our-thoughts

should even think of making the weight issue the main problem. Everything regarding this all needs to be addressed holistically, as one large-scale problem to fix. The weight is usually symptomatic of broader issues, related to one's marriage, childhood, parents, or any number of other things.

I'm about to blow your mind right here and right now. Facts don't matter. I know you are sitting there thinking that I'm completely out of my mind to suggest that. Let me prove it to you: Donald Trump is President of the United States as I sit here and type this. Donald Trump routinely wholly ignores facts, and still got elected to the Presidency. If you ever needed the proof that cognitive scientists have been saying for years, that we primarily make decisions based on emotion and confirmation bias, that should prove it to you in one fell swoop. Donald Trump is a fact-checking nightmare. Virtually everything he says is provably, technically false. This is why his opposition goes thoroughly nuts over him. They cannot stand the fact that he openly, brazenly says things that don't pass the fact-checking. Here's the kicker though: He is telling the truth, emotionally. Let me repeat that: He stretches the technical "truth," but his supporters understand that he is on their side emotionally.

Let's take the immigration issue. Early on in his campaign, he specifically stated that he was going to deport 12 million people. This served to get the immigration hardliners on his side emotionally. Over the course of his campaign, he gradually softened his immigration stance, yet retained all of his initial supporters. He had established that he was with them emotionally, then he leads them to a softer position. This is a technique called pacing and leading. He came out with the toughest position possible, got people on his side emotionally, then lead them to a softer stance. He also exaggerates virtually everything. He said that we have a 500 billion dollar trade deficit with China. It's actually in the 400 range, so it's technically a lie, but the emotional truth remains the same. China does get over on us in trade. This is how he operates because he fundamentally understands that people don't make decisions based on facts, but with emotion.

Let me illuminate your thinking further. For my next example, I'm going to use a movie that came out right as I was finishing this book: Black Panther. This is even more polarizing and exemplary of what I'm talking about than Star Wars was, but I'm going to use this movie to illustrate another lens: The Racial Lens. In the run-up to this movie, setting aside the people that didn't care, there was a racial split over this movie. A lot of white people didn't see the hype. Even a lot of Marvel fans weren't super stoked for it. On the other hand, black people were on fire like never before. I'd wager nearly every black person in the country will see this movie. Now that it's out, I don't exaggerate when I say I saw black people in tears at the end of this movie. Why is that? Their lens of life is different than that of a white person. Where you saw a movie, they saw an inspirational force for their kids with a hero that looked like them. So the lens for black people that saw this movie was as follows:

Lens 1: I am a black person.

Lens 2: I have a child.

Lens 3: Black movies usually involve slavery or humor, or negative themes.

Lens 4: Here is a nearly 100% black movie.

Lens 5: It has a hero that looks like me.

Lens 6: This hero has power, finesse, and grace, also is a king.

Lens 7: My child has a real superhero to look at that I didn't have growing up.

Now, compare that to the white person lenses:

Lens 1: I am a human.

Lens 2: I like Marvel movies and comics.

Lens 3: I will probably like this movie as well.

Notice the degree of difference of importance. For a white person, they probably just saw a cool movie, but a black person saw a different reality. They saw a degree of importance that never even crossed the white person's mind. The point to this exercise is to empower you to see the world differently and get you to understand that you have a degree of control over your mind and the lenses through which you see the world. Also, that some lenses bear radically different levels of importance to different people based on religion, race, or nationality. Once you understand how your emotions, biases, and ideology shapes how you think, it becomes much easier to see through your own bullshit, and the bullshit of others, and reach clarity of thought. This is what the Iron Mind is all about. It's not about just a diet, or going to the gym, or performing mental gymnastics to convince yourself of something. It's about a fundamental reimagining of your life and how your mind works. Once you understand that your opinion of every event you have ever witnessed is influenced by the lenses through which you saw it, you will view everything differently.

Here are the new Lenses:

Lens 1: I am a human, and I have a mind.

Lens 2: I control my mind.

Lens 3: I determine the extent to which I succeed or fail.

Lens 4: I determine how I react to things.

That's it. Those are the lenses you need to adopt, with all others coming after.

With that in mind and your lenses in place, let's get to it.

Chapter IV

Questioning the Experts

"What are you, some kind of science denier?"

These days this is the typical response to even the slightest indication that you had the temerity to question any element of anything scientific. Whether it be climate change, gender, biology, depression, or really anything, the response to even asking for evidence amounts to a nuclear meltdown.

Let me avail you of a notion: That today's science is impartial and cannot be questioned. This is not a new phenomenon. Science is not infallible. Quite the opposite. If humans are the ones doing the science, and we have built in confirmation bias about what we want to see, or the result we want to get, it is not difficult to tweak the prediction models, assumptions, and methodologies, or select ones favorable to our views. I can promise you when grant money is on the line, or career is on edge for having the wrong result, people will find a way to make the outcome what they need it to be. In the Middle Ages, someone could be put to death or imprisoned for coming to the wrong "scientific" conclusion. Today, we don't have that, but we do have loss of grant money, excommunication from the field, all for coming to the "wrong" conclusion. People like to use the term consensus or settled science. Be warned; if you hear terms like that, you are likely dealing with something that has real opposition in the scientific community, that's being repressed. No one needs to invoke consensus, or "97% agree" about gravity. The heart of the scientific method used to be that one person could disprove decades of research through provable fact. This is no longer the case. Research that comes to "unacceptable" conclusions are marginalized and repressed. Remember that Galileo was imprisoned for life for the heretical suggestion that the earth revolved around the sun.

In the 21st century, we ran into a problem we hadn't seen before: People's feelings are interfering with the scientific method. Used to, if the doctor told you to do something, you didn't argue, you just went and did it because it was accepted that the doctor knew better than you. Now, there is tremendous pressure on doctors not to attribute blame to a patient. They must find a way to not implicate the patient in the problems they are diagnosing. Everything now is categorized as a disease. Even obesity, which is a pure calorie in - calories out equation, has been twisted into something you can't help. For the past few decades, we've seen a continual push to absolve people of responsibility for their actions. Depression is another example. Let me tell you, I've had depression and know how grave it is. For several years, everyone was confident that they knew what caused depression. They were so convinced that their drug cocktails would just clean up the chemical imbalances in your brain, and you'd be good to go. Only now, after all these years, are we starting to find out that maybe, just maybe we didn't know it all about depression. It turns out; it is primarily related to things that happen to you[1], not just chemicals mingling about

---

[1] https://rootcausemedicalclinic.com/blog/depression-not-chemical-imbalance/

in your head that you can't help. ²This is what I meant earlier about science not getting it all right. The reason some of us are skeptical of scientific conclusions is very simple:

If you are older, you've seen "experts" and scientists be wrong, A LOT.

Those with the benefit of more experience have usually directly run into scenarios where the science or expert wasn't right. Then, we see things like scientists being bribed in the 60's to shift blame from sugar to fat for health issues³. We see Coke funding scientists to shift the blame for obesity away from bad diets. ⁴And these are not outliers. Everything from the nutrition, supplement, and pharmaceutical industries have been compromised in the search for profit. Let me ask you this: Have you noticed how few cures for various ailments we have these days? I couldn't even tell you the last CURE we found. Have you observed though, we have a tremendous amount of "maintenance" drugs. We have drugs for every conceivable thing, and yet somehow, few actual cures. You can now get a supplementary anti-depressant, FOR your anti-depressant. Why is this? I postulate that the pharmaceutical industry knows there is no money in curing anything. They want nothing more than for you to be on their drugs from the cradle to the grave. Fixing you doesn't help them. They want

---

² https://wakeup-world.com/2018/01/26/why-depression-is-not-caused-by-a-chemical-imbalance/
³ https://www.nytimes.com/2016/09/13/well/eat/how-the-sugar-industry-shifted-blame-to-fat.html
⁴ https://well.blogs.nytimes.com/2015/08/09/coca-cola-funds-scientists-who-shift-blame-for-obesity-away-from-bad-diets/

you convinced that their product is **necessary** for you to have, for the rest of your life. I know people on insane cocktails of drugs, who don't appear to be one iota happier than they were pre-drug. Also, it is in their interest to sell you on the fact that you can't help these things. They have managed to convince people that nothing is their fault, so they have the obvious solution, to pop a pill, every day for the rest of your life. They do not want an individual who is empowered and self-reliant, as that doesn't help them.

When I tell you scientists are full of shit a significant portion of the time, I'm not exaggerating. In my lifetime, I have watched as the nutritional guidelines have shifted from one direction to the complete opposite. Once you get to your 30's and 40's, you will have seen; in real time, experts radically shift from one side to the other. Then on top of that, the course corrections take a long time, so what ends up happening is that people don't even know the change occurred. Now, I don't consider myself a "science-denier" as I am perfectly willing to believe ironclad evidence. Faulty assumptions, methodologies, and greed can infect even the most devoted scientist. Why do I bring all this up you ask? It is vital to understand how the world messes with your Lenses of Life. Virtually no one is immune from propaganda; it is only a matter of how much of it we catch. The Iron Mind questions everything. I put this chapter up front to soften the blow for some of the things I will tell you later. There's going to be a lot of triggering, so let's continue.

Chapter V

Depression and Culture

Now it's time to prepare the trigger warning for some of my readers.

I am here to tell you, especially if you are younger, you have been deceived. You have been lied to for a significant portion of your life about a great many things. The idea that you can't help your mental faculties, that they are all in your head and just need to be taken care of with medication, is a lie. What we have currently in our society, is an epidemic of depression and mental health issues. People have been told they are depressed because of a chemical imbalance, and that all you need is an anti-depressant. It's not because you've made poor decisions that came back to haunt you, or you are dissatisfied with the state of your life. No, it's all chemicals mingling about in your head causing these problems. Part of the reason I was inspired to write this book, is seeing in society a problem of blamelessness. Every issue in one's life is somehow not their fault. Whether it's believing being fat is genetic, or depression is just brain chemicals you can't help, we have an obsession in society with not taking the blame for our problems.

Unfortunately, this mentality is now quite pervasive. We now have an entire generation who have been told that they should never experience even the slightest discomfort in any way. This is a path to sadness and misery. I will show you how to embrace the negative, and to use it to make you even more powerful than you were before. But first, you have to gain control over your mind. It's hard to reshape that which you believe you do not control. I said earlier that the chemical imbalance in your brain doesn't dictate your mindset. Chemicals do have an impact, so how can that be true? The reason it's true is that you can do things to alter the very chemicals in your brain. Numerous actions can impact what chemicals your brain and body produce. Is it not true that Endorphins from working out produce a high and good feeling? These are the realizations you must come to, that you control to a significant extent how your mind is either poisoned or enhanced. This modern idea that we don't control anything is not only absurd and untrue but damaging and dangerous as well.

For example, foods, exercise, and environment thoroughly alter brain chemistry. You can influence your mind solely based on what you eat, how you move, and the interactions you have. Coupled with some of the techniques in this book, you can make your mind your own, and power it up to incredible levels. For example, one brain chemical is Serotonin. Serotonin is a mood stabilizer that contributes to better sleep and has a positive effect on feeling good and living longer[1]. The usual point of anti-depressants is to increase Serotonin levels artificially. The downside is that they can carry side effects or just not work. Also, you aren't addressing the underlying reasons for the depression. Now, did you know that some foods contain tryptophan which can

---

[1] https://www.healthline.com/health/mental-health/serotonin#functions

increase Serotonin production?[2] It can also be influenced by exercise, sunshine, and positivity. That's right, even getting enough sun makes a difference in your body chemistry. In other words, it is possible to put your brain and body in position to generate more Serotonin, and put your biochemistry in better working order. There are many studies that link depression to obesity as well[3]. That's the point of this chapter. To make you understand that you control your mind frame. As long as you believe you aren't in control of it, you won't understand how to improve it. So changing your diet and directly addressing the reasons you are depressed can prevent depression.

At the moment of this writing, I am listening to the news report yet another school shooting, this time in Parkland, Florida. There's no word yet, but there appears to be a significant amount of fatalities. You may have noticed that school shootings are a specifically modern phenomenon. I remember in 1999 when the Columbine shooting happened. It completely blew us all away that something like that was even possible. Over the course of time since then, these have become a widespread occurrence. What changed? What is the difference Pre and Post Columbine? School shootings, unfortunately, are not the only isolated problem. Suicides, Drug use, Divorce rates are all at frequencies we've never seen before. In other words, we have a real cultural problem on our hands. In the wake of this shooting, like all others,

---

[2] https://www.healthline.com/health/healthy-sleep/foods-that-could-boost-your-serotonin

[3] https://www.everydayhealth.com/depression/depression-and-obesity.aspx

many will jump to various gun control arguments but will continue neglecting the underlying issues. People like to ascribe easy answers to complex and nuanced problems. We had tons of guns pre-1968, yet very few shootings, and certainly nothing like the various school and church shootings we have now. The guns didn't change, society changed. And not for the better. When I was growing up in the 70's and 80's, depression was barely a thing. If you were depressed, it was pretty much understood that you had life issues you needed to correct to resolve the depression. At some point in the 90's, we started to drift away from that and into the whole "It's not your fault" mantra. I know you're fat, in an unhappy marriage, and your kids hate you, but none if it is your fault. You are owed a happy life, and all you have to do is take this little pill to get your brain chemicals in order.

I believe part of the reason is the absolution we've given to people that nothing is their fault. When you absolve people of responsibility, they come to the conclusion that they are broken, and thus might as well end it all, or exist in a medication-induced stupor. Think of this: As suicide rates have risen, so too have drug abuse and medication rates. Let me clarify; I'm not characterizing all mental illness as being correctable through force of will and a robust mindset. There is a staggering amount that we as a society don't know about depression, and there are mental illnesses out there that are legitimate issues that cannot be fixed through your mental power and will. I believe those are in the minority. The overwhelming, vast majority of depressions can be overcome, without the use of medication. I've been very depressed and nearly suicidal at times. I even resorted to antidepressants at one point. I have been there, where so many before and since have been. In my younger days, I used to do some powerlifting. I was an absolute beast, extremely strong, with tons of muscle. It was all taken from me due to devastating injury, and I slipped into the depths of depression. I resorted to anti-depressants to try to fix it, and though they took a slight edge off, I was not in any way happy. It wasn't until I addressed the underlying issue head-on, that I was able to overcome it and move on. Also ironically, what caused the injury in the first place was not having mastered my mind, and overworking myself at a point when I should have stopped. Lack of mental control can manifest in many different ways, and we are going to learn how, and more importantly how to address it.

There are those, such Dr. Mark Hyman, author of the Ultramind Solution, that believes virtually every single mental issue, or as he calls them Broken Brains, is related to diet and lifestyle. I've seen enough contravening evidence to suggest that food and lifestyle aren't the cause of every single mental illness, but make absolutely no mistake: They are massive contributors, and now we are going to start looking at how. For now, understand that we can, and will learn how to manipulate your biochemistry to put your mind in the position it needs to be in to make structural changes in your life.

Let's get to it. Remember the following quote at all times:

> *"You can think your way into depression, but you have to ACT your way out."*
>
> *-George Bruno*

Chapter VI

Upgrade Your Mind

I'm going to summarize thousands of pages of research and dozens of books into one sentence that you need to understand:

You can influence your state of mind by eating correctly.

That's right, the trash you've been shoving down your gullet for years has a massive impact on your state of mind. There are innumerable books and research papers on this, such as The UltraMind Solution by Dr. Mark Hyman or Change your Brain, Change your Life by Dr. Daniel Amen. If you want to get down to the nitty-gritty of brain science, there's plenty of places you can find out which lobe controls what, which neuron fires where. I'm not here to show you which part of the brain fires when you eat a carrot. I'm skipping all of that to pound home the essence of what I'm telling you. The critical thing that you have to understand is that you are able, through food and nutrition, to directly put your brain in a healthier place. Now listen, you can achieve the Iron Mind without any specific diet because I know absolute killers that eat McDonald's virtually every day. They are outliers from the get-go. Maybe you are too, but I'm not, I need all the help I can get. There is no doubt that I perform worse in life when my diet is trash, and I'm going to show you why.

Sugar and its brethren High Fructose Corn Syrup do an incredible wrecking job on your brain. Besides screwing up your reward pathways, damaged synaptic activity, you are also talking about brain inflammation, which contributes to depression [1]. When people think of sugar or HFCS, they tend to think in terms of it making them fat. There is a lot more going on than that. I am going to pound this into your brain until it's mush: The mind and body are connected. What you feed your body will manifest in your mind. So that sugar infested dessert you pounded last night didn't just screw up your body, insulin levels, and fat, it also went straight to your brain, screwing up your serotonin and creating inflammation. And I've got even worse news: Trans fats and saturated fats are tag-teaming your brain as well. Both of these are proven to impact cognitive ability. [2]

I put this chapter up near the front of the book for a reason. It's critical that you put yourself in position to use all of the techniques I'll be introducing. By taking better care of your "Brain Health" through the right foods, you will contribute to a more positive mental state, making every single other technique more efficient. Remember, the Iron Mind is not just one element. It's many methods, habits, and perceptions all rolled into one program. I'm not here to just show you how to eat or how to think, I'm here to overhaul everything, and it starts with the junk you are likely shoving into your face.

Let's take a look. Here are a few foods with vitamins and minerals that are proven to boost your brain[3]:

---

[1] https://www.huffingtonpost.com/2015/04/06/sugar-brain-mental-health_n_6904778.html
[2] https://www.psychologytoday.com/us/blog/the-resilient-brain/201506/trans-fats-bad-your-brain
[3] https://www.webmd.com/diet/features/eat-smart-healthier-brain#1

1. Avocados (Vitamin C, E, B, K, and Folate)
2. Beets (Nitrates, Anti-Inflammatory, Boost Energy)
3. Blueberries (Vitamin C, K, and Fiber)
4. Broccoli (Vitamin C, K, and Choline
5. Dark Chocolate (Flavonols, Anti-Inflammatory, and Antioxidant)
6. Egg Yolks (Choline, Bethane Breakdown)
7. Salmon (Omega 3s)
8. Nuts (Vitamin E)
9. Whole Grains (Promotes Blood Flow)
10. Green Tea, Cocoa, Wine (Flavonoids)
11. Milk, Cereal Grains, Mushrooms (Vitamin D)
12. Red Meat, Poultry, Fish (Iron)

Now I get it, a lot of that list doesn't look super appealing. Some of you are likely thinking, "I'm not eating all that nonsense, I like my trash diet." Well, you had better figure out how bad you want the life you dream about, because guess what: It's not easy. Don't worry though, I'm going to introduce you to some tactics to get around eating healthy 24/7 and allow you to eat cheat meals once in awhile. Don't think of these in a vacuum. You don't have to sit there and eat a ton of beets in one fell swoop. Learn to get innovative. Trust me, I think beets and broccoli taste like trash, but I learned to spice them up. For me, I eat a ton of broccoli because I figured out how to make it not be terrible without adding a bunch of calories by using Lemon Juice. Salmon is the same way. I'm here to tell you right now that salmon is one of the Iron Foods. It is almost impossible to be better food than salmon. Honestly, If you could eat salmon every day, that would be awesome. Another trick is to learn to make smoothies, and I don't mean dessert drinks, actual healthy smoothies. Part of having the Iron Mind is not deluding ourselves. And you know when you have most smoothies that they are basically a dessert. Don't lie to yourself.

In the diet section, we will get more in depth, but for now understand that when I say you control your mind to an astonishing degree, this is what I'm talking about. It's not just a bunch of mental tricks, the things you put in your body absolutely have an impact on your mental state. Do I eat junk food occasionally? Yes, I do. I'm not sitting here on high acting like you have to have a pristine diet handed down from Mt. Olympus to develop an Iron Mind. I have about 7-8 items on that list that I rotate around, and I definitely cheat once in a blue moon. We will talk about cheating later, and the vital role I believe it plays. For now, understand that we are doing one thing right now:

Setting you up to win.

Chapter VII

Music: The Ultimate Weapon

"Music produces a kind of pleasure which human nature cannot do without."

-Confucius

I never truly understood the power of music when I was growing up. My Dad listened to all manner of country music, and my Mom Adult Contemporary. Now, let me preface this by saying there's some astonishing music in those two genres. I love artists like Brooks and Dunn, Alan Jackson, Keith Whitley in the country genre. On the adult contemporary side, artists like Bryan Adams, Rod Stewart, and Phil Collins are amazing. However, none of these artists ever spoke to me. I never felt any of it move my soul. Virtually every song I listened to growing up, was some variant of a few things:
1. Crying about women or relationships.
2. Getting drunk or partying.
3. Talking about love.

Those themes encompassed probably 90+% of what I was listening. There is nothing wrong with those themes in music. There is some phenomenal music with those themes, some that can even be used with the techniques I will lay out for you. Music is highly personal to the individual. You must find what stirs your soul. In your pursuit of a more positive life and powerful mind, music is a weapon. I would argue, it might be one of the most potent weapons in your arsenal.

For me, that musical weapon is Heavy Metal.

Growing up in the religious community, heavy metal had an awful reputation. Especially in the small Baptist Christian school from which I graduated. It was considered devil music, something to be afraid of that would lead one to Satan. Shy boy that I was, I was almost scared of it. Bands like Slayer and Motley Crue actually scared me with their over the top album covers. I would go into music stores and slink past the metal section with its pentagrams and demon head covers, like a dog shirking from its master after it had done something wrong. I remember the Parents Council war on Metal, and how they were so sure it convinced people to commit suicide and worship the devil. They tried to say that "backmasking" aka playing something backward had some disturbing content, enticing the user to commit suicide or worship Satan. Looking back, it sounds insane now, but back then it was a real concern. I remember Rob Halford of Judas Priest answering these questions. They accused Priest of saying "Do it" on a backmask recording, enticing the listener to commit suicide, and Halford denied it and simply responded "Do what? Mow the lawn?" He then asked why they would entice their fan base to kill themselves, as that would be the worst way to promote an album of all time. So metal had a terrible reputation, and I bought into the mass hysteria. I heard some of it occasionally and was convinced it was nonsense, no talent gibberish. I remember one guy in 5th grade snuck a Motley Crue tape into school and we all huddled over it like it was some kind of drug level contraband.

Once I got out of school, I let myself open up a bit. I started growing my hair out, hanging out with friends more and gaining new ones. In other words, I was ready to hear something new. As I mentioned earlier, ending up in my friends truck listening to Slayer started it all. For the first time, I was hearing music that told me I could be powerful, that I could stand tall, that I could be more than I was. That was the message I got from Heavy Metal. The themes from my previous music were themes of love, supplicating to women, drinking and partying. Now, I was hearing themes of power, domination, strength, ambition, heroism, and elevating oneself. Even now as I think back to those times, I find it astounding what music has done for my life. I can honestly say that I'm not sure I would be sitting here if not for the power of music, and more specifically, heavy metal. When someone asked me about the things that have changed my life and made me happy, metal is at the very top of the list, possibly even number one. I'm not even sure I'd be alive if it weren't for Heavy Metal.

Around this time is where I started to understand the power of music. I read all the lyrics and found the songs that had the most powerful lyrics, coupled with the most powerful music. I memorized them and repeated them to myself. People were astounded that I knew the lyrics to virtually everything. To this day, I have over 20,000 metal songs in my library, and I have the lyrics to every single one. For me, it was never enough for the song to sound cool. I needed it to be saying something that was powerful. This is where Pantera came in. They were my first love in the world of music. I worshipped Pantera in those days. My snake tattoo on my arm comes from one of their albums. Virtually every song was a powerhouse of might and determination. I can, without hyperbole, say that the song "Becoming" quite literally changed my life. As I mentioned earlier, this was also around the time I started working out. So, I was now working on the stronger body, and power fueled my mind.

I cannot stress enough how critical lyrics are to your success. I know people that have listened to a song dozens of times, and still, have no idea what's being said. By doing this, you are leaving tremendous power on the table. I know songs that sound great, but either has vapid or unimportant lyrics. I will not have such a song in my playlist. For a song to make my playlist, it has to have both. Generally, I don't like instrumentals at all, unless it's for relaxation. To work out without powerful lyrics is leaving half of your potential power on the table. If you want to go to war, you don't go by leaving the Air Force behind and only sending in ground troops. You need to use all available weapons to feed the Iron Mind. The songs that have pushed me to the greatest heights have the combination of tremendous instrumentation and melody, with amazing vocals and powerful, empowering lyrics. These are the only songs that make my serious playlist, especially for working out. I will share this playlist of mine, and completely different ones that others use at the end of this book.

Here is a trick I learned very early on, that I had no idea I was doing. I learned early, in small part, how to reframe my mind. I know how to do this now consciously, but back then I just kind of picked it up. What I would do, is I would take a song I liked the music to, and insert myself into it, and take even a negative lyric and make it positive. Say I was listening to a Slayer song that involved the horrors of the military industrial complex and war. I would insert myself into the battlefield. I would imagine that I was on the battlefield slaying hordes of enemies. This mental technique, coupled with working out, drove me. I learned to power myself up to the point that I felt I could make my blood boil. As I looked down at the veins in my arms during a workout, I imagine my veins thundering and pulsing with power. We will talk more about projection and reframing techniques in a later chapter.

> *"Music is like is a legal drug for athletes,"*
>
> -Costas Karageorghis, Ph.D.,

It turns out; there are a lot of studies on this[1]. Music thoroughly engages your mind[2]. It is proven science that music improves performance at various activities compared directly with listening vs. not listening. Brain scans reveal that music engages the brain[3], and fires up the areas that involve memory, attention, planning, and emotion. Music fires up the Dopamine levels in our brain, the chemical responsible for pleasure. This is part of what I was referring to in the previous chapter. You can definitely, purposefully, influence whats going on in your head. This recent progressive idea that things just happen to us, that it's all out of our control, is nonsense. Study after study proves we can influence our brain, and music is absolutely a prime mover. As I mentioned before, we can alter our brain, on purpose. If you haven't found the music

---

[1] https://www.healthline.com/health-news/mental-listening-to-music-lifts-or-reinforces-mood-051713
[2] https://med.stanford.edu/news/all-news/2007/07/music-moves-brain-to-pay-attention-stanford-study-finds.html
[3] http://www.medicaldaily.com/your-brain-music-how-our-brains-process-melodies-pull-our-heartstrings-271007

that moves you, keep looking. There are dozens of genres and even more subgenres within. Within metal alone, I can name over 40 subgenres, all with different themes and melody. Think of what inspires you, then find the music that plays to that inspiration. If you discover that Arnold Schwarzenegger inspires you for example, and you like action movies, there's actually a band for that. Austrian Death Machine is an Arnold inspired metal band, which uses his films and quotes as a basis for their music. So when I say you can find something that invigorates you, even if it's insanely and oddly specific, I mean it.

Now, I will admit something I've never told any of my metalhead friends, and probably not to anyone in public. I love some of Katy Perry's and Lady Gaga's music. That's right, I admit it, a metal head with the guilty pleasure of a few mainstream pop artists. Roar and Bad Romance are two amazing songs that work great for this purpose. Never limit yourself, there's always wealth to mine even in music you don't generally like. Here's another example, I absolutely hate Rap and Hip Hop for the most part. As a miscellaneous white guy, I don't identify with many of the themes, nor do I like the beats of the music. However, my ultimate workout playlist has precisely ONE rap song. That honor goes to DMX with "X Gonna Give It To Ya." I generally hate rap and hip-hop, but I have been able to pull a few gems from DMX, MOP, and Eminem. Being closed minded isn't helping us in pursuit of the Iron Mind. For you, Beethoven might be a primary driver. Possibly Clint Black. I even know people like Henry Rollins, a famous punk musician with Black Flag, who listen to ballads while lifting weights to feel more emotionally connected to themselves as they work out. The point is, whatever moves you, whatever drives you, you have to make a concerted effort to use that power constructively. Mentally acknowledge it, and strategize how best to implement the weapon known as music into your life to improve your mindset.

Here's my strategy:

On a work out day, I make sure I've started by taking a brisk walk with the dog. During this walk, I generally say my affirmation (We will discuss affirmations later) and I do a breathing exercise. I used to get winded and out of breath quickly before I learned to breathe correctly (which I will explore in a later chapter). Do just enough walking to get a little movement and blood flow. I go home, get dressed and head out to the gym. In the car, I play something lighter and super catchy. Get your head bobbing and maybe sing along. Once I'm at the gym, I have to warm up, so this is where we still keep it light. Some upbeat classical works great for this, but some slightly lighter metal works too. Now I start the weights. This is where we increase the pace and ferocity. We venture into a bit heavier territory here, but make sure you save the really heavy artillery for later when you start getting tired. The most powerful stuff you have, you want to preserve for those exhausting sets. When you are arriving at your limits, this is where you bring out the big guns. For me it's Nile. I know all of their lyrics, and the most potent songs, so they come out when I need nuclear weapons to finish a workout.

Think of it in terms of a battle. If you are going to war over something small, you don't drop a nuclear bomb first. You might send in the ground troops or a drone strike. As the intensity of the war escalates, so too do your tactics. Now you are using F22 fighter jets and Abrams tanks. And when the war is nigh unwinnable, you drop the big MOAB bombs. Then, if all else fails, you go for the Nuclear weapon when all else is lost. This is the strategy. Know what your big guns are regarding music, and use them strategically. On my last, most exhausting maximum effort set, that's where User-Maat-Re by Nile comes in. It's a long song and starts slow. The slow beginning allows you to catch your breath for a moment and reflect on the conquest to come. The song is about Ramses II, and how he had to build grander more spectacular monuments and was driven to have more dominating conquests than his father, Seti I. During the song, as Ramses establishes his empire and vanquishes his enemies, I am embarking on a conquest of my own. As he reaches the zenith of his power, so too do I. Some of my most satisfying accomplishments in the gym have occurred with Ramses by my side and in my head. As he conquered, so do I. As Ramses spills the blood of his enemies, my blood is boiling and thundering with purpose.

So do I use the same themes everywhere? Certainly not. As incredible as Nile is for workouts, I learned it isn't the best before I go to work. I've found that I can not only use music to power me up in the gym, but also to calm and soothe. Remember, I said to look at the things that you love, that inspire, relax, and motivate you, and find artists and bands that feed those things. This is how I discovered a group called Agalloch. I am most at home in the woods. I love the serenity and peace nature provides. As I type this, I have my window open and look to the vast forest outside. I feel the light breeze of a fall day, with the limbs of ancient trees swaying. I hear nothing but the breeze, the birds, and nature. I discovered Agalloch many years ago, but never seriously listened to them because I was still in the city and hadn't yet realized my love of nature. So even though I had them available, I wasn't at a point in time where they would speak to me. Now, they reside in the pantheon of my favorite bands of all time. On a brisk fall day, I feel most at peace near the woods, with Agalloch permeating my mind.

I talked to a friend of mine about music one time. Now, for a little background, he's pretty depressive and sad a lot. He doesn't work out, walks around like a zombie, and has very little ambition in life. One day I asked him "Hey man let me see your music on your phone." He handed it over, and I scanned his playlist. Virtually everything he had was depressive, sad, and emotional, music. Knowing him as I did, his choice of music didn't surprise me in the least. He was in a vicious circle of being depressed, then feeding that depression, which only served to make him more depressed. What we play matters. I heard a parable once called Two Wolves. The parable goes like this:

One evening an old Cherokee told his grandson about a battle that goes on inside people.

He said, ' My son, the battle is between two ' wolves ' inside us all.

One is Evil. - It is anger, envy, jealousy, sorrow, regret, greed, arrogance, self-pity, guilt, resentment, inferiority, lies, false pride, and ego.

The other is Good. - It is joy, strength, peace, love, hope, serenity, humility, kindness, benevolence, empathy, generosity, truth, compassion and faith. '

The grandson thought about it for a minute and then asked his grandfather:

'Which wolf wins? '

The old Cherokee simply replied, ' The one you feed.'

The music you use to feed your mind makes a difference. If you are listening to weak, depressive music, it will feed that part of your mind. You must feed the Good Wolf inside. Feed it with the right messages, the messages of strength, determination, joy, or serenity. So do I ever listen to negative themes? Yes absolutely. Sometimes during a foggy, grey, or rainy day, I do. I do however make a concerted effort to keep those themes to a minimum. Every once in awhile though, I absolutely do listen to themes of love, loss, heartbreak, or sadness. I just try to maintain a balance. Keep things positive the majority of the time. During this book at periodic times, you will come across a small excerpt of some of my favorite artists. I'll detail how I use them, and their most powerful songs. I implore you to do the same. Henry Rollins once said, "The best way to fight weakness is with strength." Find the theme, the artists, learn the lyrics, and use them to build your Iron Mind.

Music is distilled power.

Learn to use it.

Chapter VIII

The Toxicity Audit

What the heck is a toxicity audit? It's an inventory of all the items in your life that are adding a toxic element, and thus degrading your attempts at building the Iron Mind. We are a social species. We are meant to gather together, socialize, procreate, and interact. It is in our nature to want, and need love and companionship. However, you must come to a terrible realization: You likely need to eliminate people and habits from your life, as some are toxic to your mental health. One might think this is obvious, but very few follow up and do it. I am here to tell you that it is challenging to get to where you want to go if you have these things poisoning your mind along the way. In this case, what we want to do is improve our lives, and develop an Iron Mind. This process will be aided by removing the toxic elements from your life. If they are inhibiting your development and making you miserable, then they have to go.

Any leader will tell you that one of the most complicated areas of their job is firing people. Even when someone absolutely deserves it, it can be very tricky to get rid of someone. Breakups are even worse. Breaking contact with someone you needed or loved in the past is extremely difficult. One thing I can tell you with 100% certitude though: Sometimes it has to be done. We all have someone, probably multiple people that we have had to let go for a variety of reasons. What I'm encouraging you to do right now is what I call a "Toxicity Audit." What I mean by that, is evaluating everyone and everything you interact with regularly, and take stock of what value they add to your life.

Do I get stressed when this person is around?

Is this music introducing negative themes?

Is this person continually asking for favors?

Are they a distraction from my goals?

Do I look forward to seeing this person?

What value do we add to each other's life?

Is this person talking me out of things that are beneficial to me?

Does this person treat me with respect?

Is this habit helping or hindering me?

These are just a few of the questions you need to ask about every single person and element in your life. This is going to be an extremely tough process, as we all have things that we know don't add value to our lives, but for which we have some sentimental connection to, so we keep them around. I am here to tell you that you are only hurting yourself by doing this. As it relates to people, you could be damaging them by enabling the toxic behavior. If you have a friend who is an alcoholic, is it helpful to them to go to the bar with them regularly? Of course not.

I'm going to tell you a mind-blowing secret: You don't have to be friends with people you don't like. And to take that a step further, the people you interact with ARE Future You. Let that one sink right in for a second. As you are growing up, you become a composite of the people you are around the most, that exert the most influence over you. We are going to talk a lot more about Future You later on, but for now, understand that you are who you surround yourself with. You gradually take on their characteristics, mannerisms, sayings, and habits. Think about it, as you grew up, what was once "peer pressure" in a lot of cases just became part of you. This is why the Toxicity Audit is so critical. You have to recognize the long-term effects of the people and habits in your sphere. One thing I've done my whole life is eliminate people from my world that cause drama. If someone is bringing toxic behavior into my life, then they are going to be gone. It is that simple. I have had the unfortunate task of excommunicating some previously great friends from my life. Now, I'm not suggesting to be heartless. If you have someone that's been a friend for 30 years, that's having some issues you don't just bail on them. You should still do what you can to help them, but realize some people can't be helped. Some people are what they are, and won't change, or have to hit bottom for a change to be made. What I'm saying to do, is give it a world-class effort to help, but make sure to draw the line at some point. You cannot be an enabler of their toxic behavior, nor can you accept that impact on your life for very long.

Keep in mind as well; this doesn't just include alcoholics and druggies. I've had to purge friends that were neither. If someone is adding stress or taking value from your time and life, then they have to go. I've unfortunately had to remove two long term friends from my life. One, who I'll call Bob, was a friend for over a decade that I spent countless hours with. Bob wasn't a drunk or druggie, but he was a colossal asshole and took a lot of value from others. Bob was always number one to himself and anyone that even remotely intruded on that he invariably had a snarky line for. Also, he always had to have his way. He would argue endlessly about which restaurant or place he wanted to go. My other friends and I would eventually give in just to avoid more confrontation. On top of all that, he thrived on that confrontation. Friends, family, it didn't matter. He got off on getting his way and being right, and he'd go out of his way to make it happen, even over the most trivial matters. It bothered me for a long time, and I eventually decided that my life would be better without him. I still have other friends that associate with him once in awhile, and they never fail to complain about something he's done to take value from others. Every time I hear these stories, I realize I did make the right decision all those years ago.

Another friend who I'll call Jim had a different set of issues. He grew up in a hardcore Christian family and went to the same Christian school with me. We started in second grade together and were friends all the way up till our 3rd or the 4th year out of high school. He began to rebel somewhat early on and was a constant source of trouble. Be it drinking, stealing, or cheating he always had something nefarious going on. I remember an incident where I went to a Roses department store with Jim and his group of troublemakers. There was four of us, and I knew going in that they were looking to do some shoplifting. I was never one for criminality, so I held off on stealing anything. As I was leaving the store, a massive security guard ran up and got in my face and yelled: "which one is Jim?" Jim was standing right over by the car in front, and the security guy went after him and hauled him into the back of the store. He asked me if I had anything that belonged to him, and I said I didn't. They were eventually hauled out in handcuffs, and I walked away free. That's just one incident out of too many to recount. Looking back, I'm amazed he's not dead. Even after losing his best friend in an alcohol-fueled car wreck, he still never changed. He drank heavily and did a lot of drugs, and I tried like hell for years to get him to stop. He once came over to my apartment unmistakably drunk and proceeded to put cigarette ashes all over my floor. Every time he came around, it was always some drama. I pleaded with him to let me help, trying to convince him to go to the gym with me, and he never did. The cycle of self-destruction continued unabated for years.

Both of these cases are people I loved for a long time. I gave both of them a hell of an effort to help, but I realized after a time and monumental struggle that neither could be. At least not by me. This was during my reformation periods in my life, and I had to make tough decisions. Now I sit here at 40, with a fabulous life and absolutely no drama, and I think back to the people I've had to lose in my life. Everyone that I've removed from my life has brought me to a point where I'm really content. There is not a shred of doubt in my mind that I would not be in the position I am now had I kept some of the toxic people around. They poison your mind and prevent you from reaching your full potential. You need to keep people in your life that add value and make you happy.

Included in this policy, I also include family and significant others. Being of the same blood or marriage does not give them license to add stress and tribulation to your life. Clearly, these are going to be the most difficult. The hardest thing I've ever had to do was break up with someone that was in love with me. She is a great woman to this day, but I didn't love her. It would have been cruel to continue to give her the hope that I was the one when I knew otherwise. Sometimes, even when you really like someone, they have to be gone, not only for your benefit but theirs too. This can require you to really look at yourself as well, not just your friends and family. If you aren't adding value to their life, if you know you can't provide them with what they want, then you have to do the right thing and remove yourself.

Let's talk a bit more about dating. This is an area that I feel especially solid about, and one that I believe I've mastered over the years. Let me reduce this down to one rule for simplicity sake. If you follow this one rule, you will be successful in dating. The rule is as follows: If I get one whiff of drama, I'm out. It's that simple. And by drama, I don't mean if we have one argument I break up with someone. I mean really look at their life and how chaotic it is. Do not bring someone into your life that is going to bring chaos and drama into it. Google and Facebook EVERYONE. I can't stress this enough. Virtually everyone you meet is going to have some online footprint. Some might call this stalking; I call it extreme vetting. I do not play around with skanks, sluts, or inferior partners. If I get even the slightest red flag, I'm gone. Now, this essentially means you will only be going for the best. That's fine. If you have the Iron Mind, you will have the confidence to do just that. Even being rejected multiple times in a row won't faze you, you just soldier forward. Now, this doesn't mean you search for perfection. I've dated many non-perfect women in my life. It's not perfection you seek; it's value. You are looking for someone who adds value to your life. I'll delve further into this in a later chapter, but understand that toxic relationships have to go as well.

So what did I do wrong with the people in my life? No question I've made errors. Several. First, I allowed working out to dominate my life to a degree that wasn't healthy. For the better part of 10 years, I didn't even try to talk to women or increase my network or skill set. I was essentially a hermit, who only worked, went to the gym, and played World of Warcraft. Secondly, back in my shy days, I was told directly by a female I really liked that I just wasn't confident enough. The shyness and lack of confidence really ruined a couple of potential relationships. I also have been historically terrible at networking and making new friends. I can tell you 100% that you have to get good at this. Building a network I used to view as a shallow operation, and I couldn't have been more wrong. This is a critical aspect of moving forward and gaining new opportunities. Do not underestimate its value.

No conversation about toxicity would be complete without talking about what could be a primary driver: Your job. I've been there, in a job I hated that I spent even my time off complaining about and fretting over. The work you do is one of the central pillars of your life. If this part is wrong, and causing problems or drama, it will poison the rest of your life at a level that is almost impossible to overstate. The wrong job can poison your mind to a degree that is difficult to match. Now I'm not advising you to immediately quit because you don't like your job. What I am proposing is to prepare to leave. If you are one of these people, stuck in a job you hate, now is the time to get ready for a change. I've made the mistake of walking out of a job I wasn't ready to leave. I've also done it the right way. This last time I did it, I was ready. I had the funds, the infrastructure, the design, and the plan all ready to go before I did it. I had a 33 point checklist of items I wanted to be done before I left, and the day I hit them all, I called my boss and put in my two weeks. Have a plan to move on. It might seem like too much, you might have a family or kids to care for, and I understand that. You are never trapped. Update your resume, improve your skillset, and get really good at networking and persuasion. Read the books by Dale Carnegie and Robert Cialdini. You can get out. Feeling trapped in a dead end for the next 20 years is a terrible feeling. Do what you need to do to either step it up, or get out of a dead end, soul-sucking job.

Now, if you are only going for the high tier people or even jobs, there will be competition. This is why you must follow the principles in this book. If you are going to date high tier individuals or go for high tier jobs, you must be in the upper tier yourself. If you are mediocre, you will attract mediocrity. That's why it's critical to put all of the pieces into play. Remember, 80% of people are competing for the top 20%. Are you going to be the one that gets into the top 20%, or the one that settles for the bottom 80%? This is why it's crucial to bring every weapon you have into the war of life.

When it comes to bad habits, I had a few myself during my personal growth days. I smoked cigarettes like a machine, even when I was working out. I'd have a cigarette first thing before and after the gym. I had overly unhealthy workout habits, going to the gym far too much. I played way too many video games, especially World of Warcraft, a game I lived and breathed for over eight years. We will talk more about games later, believe me. Now, on the plus side, these were all minimal habits in terms of scale compared to something like drug or alcohol abuse. However, an addiction is an addiction, regardless of the level of harm. Whether its gambling or video games, the principle remains the same. Keep in mind the entire point of most drugs or addictions is the Dopamine spike in your brain. I talked about Serotonin earlier and how it contributes to a sense of well being. Well, guess what, low Serotonin levels increase the motivation to acquire Dopamine. So in other words, if you aren't happy, you are going to seek out ways to spike that Dopamine more vigorously. This is what I meant in earlier chapters about everything between the mind and body being tied together. You must view your living state holistically. Holistically is a word I used to hate because it seemed to get thrown around and placed in vague context. In this context, we use it to refer to how we view ourselves as one organism. Mind, Body, Spirit. Neglect one, the others are likely to falter.

You have to move past these habits that frame your world. Quitting smoking was insanely difficult. I smoked for 16 years, and I loved smoking. I didn't want to quit. I viewed it as an excellent relaxer and a free break at work. The reason I ended up stopping was the financial impact, as cigarettes kept getting progressively more expensive. Also, I worked out a lot, and smoking really harmed my lung capacity. So even though I enjoyed it and didn't want to quit, I invented reasons to do it and rationalized why it was necessary. You see, I could afford them, and I was still insanely strong while smoking. This is all mental reframing technique, which we will address later. Find a reason to quit, then purposefully amplify that reason in your mind. This is where you really have to have other things lined up to help. Whatever excuse you need to make to stop, whether it be family, the gym, money, health, just take that excuse and make a list of reasons to stop. Cement them in your mind and instantly turn to them in tough times. Also, establish rituals, which I will detail later. Rituals and routine can really do a lot to help battle addiction. If you are sitting around bored, you are going to be more likely to think about the addictive item.

The other part is that you have to believe in your will. You have to believe your will can trump the addiction. This is why I spent a lot of time in the first chapters talking about the degree to which you control your mind and the lenses we place on life. Thousands have beaten addiction without drugs, and you can too. You just have to believe you can. Belief, coupled with the right practices, can move mountains. This is why the current narratives of absolving responsibility are so dangerous. If you don't believe in your own will, you will have a difficult time overcoming it. Just remember that millions before you have beaten personal demons, and they did it without pharmaceuticals. The right strategy, the right rituals, and the right attitude will overcome. Learn to terminate with extreme prejudice:

Hear a negative song? Gone from the playlist.

See a negative Tweet? Unfollowed.

Let nothing poison your mind.

Eliminate it all, and you will be better off for it.

Chapter IX

A Systemic Overhaul

As far back as I can remember, I've always hated setting goals. Especially in my work life, I constantly did everything I could to avoid them. Everything from "You need to sell X amount of this" or "I need to lose X amount of weight" always bothered me. For some reason, I always hated the idea of incremental goals like that. I never had a problem with an overarching vision for your life, such as "Hey I want to be an astronaut one day." I never had a problem with that type of goal. But I always hated day to day or week to week goals. Here are a few reasons why:

Once you hit the goal, you are very likely to start slacking off. As I will address in the diet chapter, diets fail because people actually hit the dieting goal, and then stop. It's been the same throughout my work career. I've observed hundreds of people get a goal for the day, say to sell X amount of dollars, and nearly 95% of the time, once they hit the goal, they go right into slacker mode. I've caught myself doing this a lot early in my career. I'd say to myself "I gotta do 10 of this that or the other thing today". Invariably, one of two results would come of it:
1. I'd hit it, then slack off after.
2. I didn't hit it; then I was miserable the rest of the day.

Goals are a bitch like that. There's generally an issue, whether or not you hit it. But I'm going to tell you the biggest reason I hate goals:

You exist in a state of perpetual failure until you accomplish the goal.

This was the part I really hated about setting goals. It always felt like I was losing, right up until I hit the goal. Personally, I always preferred to be in a constant state of improvement, rather than to set a goal and then fall off after. So, instead of setting goals, I just set about doing things correctly in perpetuity. I never had a name for it, but Scott Adams provided one: Systems vs. Goals. So, he was able to classify something I had been doing for years, but never really articulated. In other words, it's far better to put the correct systems in place, than to just set a goal. This is why people have such a big problem with diets. To them, the diet is just a miserable mechanism to get to a specific goal weight. Thus, once that weight is achieved, its back to eating large pizzas again. So here's how I break it down:

Goal: Lose 20 pounds.

System: Learn to eat healthier, and continue it on an ongoing basis and work in cheat meals as rewards.

In the diet section, I'll go over a lot more. The point is, however, to reframe your mind into an ongoing thing that's beneficial to you, instead of setting a goal that will make you miserable the entire time you are after it. Here's another one:

Once I started my Twitter account, I immediately set a goal of 100 new followers a month. I would go a day or two without a new follower and freak out and start sweating that I wasn't going to make the arbitrary goal I had set for myself. I would have been better off setting the right processes in place, like more engaging tweets, smarter use of hashtags, and better content, rather than sitting there and freaking out that I wasn't meeting some random number I picked out of the sky. Remember, if you are doing things the right way, then the results will come. I find the New England Patriots to be a great example of this. They have a famous quote that is amazing in its simplicity:

"Do your Job."

-Bill Belichick

That is the essence of systems vs. goals. The idea Belichick has is that if everyone on the team does their job correctly, across 54 people, then winning will happen. So he and his staff focus on process and fundamentals, rather than placing his team in a perpetual state of failure until they hit some arbitrary goal. Sure you have an ending, overarching goal of winning the Super Bowl and to win every game, but they aren't the focus of his training or day to day activity. I know people who are goal setters and have been successful doing so. Part of it is learning how you work most efficiently and doing that thing. So, I would suggest picking one or the other. For me systems work best, but if you find that you are especially motivated by pressure then by all means set goals.

Understanding which works best for you is what matters, but you need to understand we aren't here to lose weight. Do not create a goal that puts you in a losing frame of mind, ever. We are here to change our lives, forever. To do this, we need to put permanent systems in place that allow us to establish discipline and ritual. We will talk more about ritualizing things later, but for now, understand how necessary it is to put the right practices in place.

Your goal is not to lose 20 pounds any longer. It is to overhaul your life and create the conditions necessary to maintain your ideal life.

Forever.

Chapter X

Become What You Are

"He who has a why to live for can bear almost any how."

-Friedrich Nietzsche

Nietzsche has had a significant influence on me. Ever since I read the Anti-Christ, Thus Spake Zarathustra, and Beyond Good and Evil, I've thought a lot about morality and becoming the best version of oneself. How to ascend to the highest plateau of humanity, and unlock the power of the mind. Some of his ideas like master-slave morality can be very thought-provoking and controversial. Even his concept of the "Overman," Super Man, or Ubermensch has been taken and attributed to Nazi ideology, mostly as a result of his sister after he died. Put into its most simple frame the idea of the Overman is an ascendant human, that transcends race, religion, or ideology. Nietzsche viewed race, religion, country, and even morality as beneath the Overman. This is why the Overman concept is not inherently racial, as Nazi propaganda might suggest. Personally, I believe anyone, of any race or religion, can be that ascendant human. This also goes hand in hand with his other concept: The Will to Power. I will discuss this at length as well, as I believe the knowledge and understanding of these concepts contribute to the goal of developing the Iron Mind.

Become what you are. What does that even mean? My definition is that everyone has an inherent potential for something good, great, or even world-changing.

Here's the funny thing about potential though: It means a grand total of nothing. If you don't embrace it and push to take what you want out of life, then all the potential in the world means absolutely nothing. Clearly, not everyone has the talent or ability to become the next Michael Jordan or Steve Jobs, but the question is, are we the best possible version of what we are capable? What is the limit of your human potential? Somewhere, there is a person that's likely smarter, stronger, or has greater potential than all of us, undiscovered due to either their circumstances or more likely, their limitations placed on themselves of what they can be. They can't become what they are because they can't remove the mental blocks and self-doubt standing in their way. Make no mistake; this isn't just about lowly individuals, someone might even be famous, and still not reach their maximum potential. Also, there's another way to look at this. The saying is "Become WHAT you are." I take that to mean that to live your best life; it's necessary to find what it is that you are intended to do. I spent a lot of years just aimlessly floating through life, from one job to the next. I always had a sense of restlessness and apathy, mostly because I was doing mediocre work that wasn't what I was supposed to be doing. Now, I was still doing that mediocre work pretty well, but my heart was never really in it because I subconsciously knew it wasn't what I was supposed to be doing. Then on top of all of that, it's almost impossible to give all of yourself and apply the maximum level of will, if you aren't doing what works best for you.

Let me tell you a secret: It is easy to be mediocre. It's easy to sit and binge Netflix shows instead of doing the hard work necessary to become what you are. Mediocrity is a gravitational vortex. It sucks you in, and you have to battle your way out. The fight is long and arduous, and you'll find yourself questioning everything along the way. In our modern society, everything exists to make our lives easier. Addictions are plentiful, and in some cases, cheap or even free. Becoming what you are is not going to just happen, you have to engage in battle every step of the way to make true your future reality. Someone out there at this very moment is giving it everything they have. You have to be willing to forge yourself in the crucible of combat to become the Future You that you envision.

How then do we find out what it is we are supposed to be doing? It took me decades to figure things out, I was quite literally 39 years old and didn't have a clear vision. Part of the reason I was so aimless through life, was that I never really tried new things. I settled into my mediocre rut of life, and never set myself outside my comfort zone to try new things. If you told me even two years ago I'd be sitting here writing this book; I would have laughed in your face. You have to try new things regularly to discover the buried truths about yourself and what is it that you are supposed to "become." To become what you are also requires removing obstacles in your path, that limit what you can be. These obstacles can include, but are not limited to:
1. Jealousy and Envy
2. Toxic Relationships
3. Physical Weakness
4. Self Loathing

5. Inconsistency
6. Criticism of Others
7. Drugs and Alcohol
8. Self Doubt
9. Excuses
10. Financial Instability

These are but a few of the obstacles we must overcome. Think of it like this, the more talent one has, the fewer of those they have to worry about. For those of us that are pretty standard, non-savant humans, we have to combat virtually all of them to be our best. Some of those items are bigger deals than others. For example, drugs and alcohol can wreck everything by themselves. How many people that could have been the absolute best of all time at something have been ruined by drugs and alcohol? I haven't addressed these substances yet, so let's take a look at their impact.

Personally, I don't do any drugs, and I can't even remember the last time I was drunk. I do have a delicious hard cider on a crisp fall day once in awhile, but that's the extent of my drinking. For myself, I like to stay 100% percent sharp at all times, and anything that distorts or dulls my senses is not something I'm interested in. These can singlehandedly ruin you, by themselves. I'm not even in favor of marijuana, despite the fact that I don't even believe there's anything wrong with it. Honestly, I think marijuana is leagues better than alcohol, to the point where there's no comparison. That being said, I still don't think marijuana should be legal; and yes, I'm aware of the seeming contradiction of that statement.

Here's my argument against marijuana and the reason I don't believe you should do it. I know people who perform at an extremely high level, while smoking tremendous amounts of weed, such as Michael Phelps, The Diaz brothers, Joe Rogan, and others. That is the extreme minority though. For the vast majority of people, marijuana is a one-way ticket to the laziness vortex. We already have a problem in our society of lazy disengagement. Legalizing Weed just provides yet another vice to contribute to the denigration of our culture. I can agree on medical application, but as a recreational drug, I am not a fan. Now, that doesn't mean YOU can't perform and be great on it, but I really don't recommend it. Also, it contributes considerably to another of the issues mentioned earlier, and that is financial stability. I know people who quite literally spend hundreds of dollars a month on either weed or alcohol. Finances can create a tremendous amount of stress, so ignore it at your peril. Remember, we do want to reduce stress as much as possible, but still stay sharp and sober.

As for alcohol, I'm not a fan as I just generally hate the taste, and as I mentioned before, I hate not staying sharp. In addition, I have watched friends die, and waste away due to alcohol. Alcohol is one of the worst offenders in preventing the Iron Mind. It negatively contributes to chaos, finances, health, far too many areas to be of use. Now, I do believe that it is possible for one to drink socially and stay on track IF you have the discipline to be able to regulate yourself. Since we are trying to develop a powerful mind, I would recommend staying away altogether. We want to avoid sabotaging ourselves when we aren't entirely alert, and alcohol can absolutely ruin us while under the influence.

One example of becoming what you are against all the odds is in the story of Audie Murphy. In the World War 2 era, he was undersized and underweight and had his sister forge an affidavit so he could join the army a year earlier than he should have. This small man would become one of the greatest American heroes of all time. Reading his list of heroics makes Rambo look like a documentary. He won virtually every award there is to win, including the Medal of Honor. After slaying dozens of Nazis, numerous heroic acts, and promotions, upon return he found he had PTSD, known back then as "Shell-Shock" or "Combat Fatigue." It haunted him and nearly made him suicidal. He took sleeping pills to help him combat it and eventually became addicted. He then decided to lock himself in a hotel room for a week, to break the addiction. He did successfully beat the addiction and went on to become a writer and actor, and PTSD activist. It is chiefly because of his activism in 1971 that PTSD started to be taken more seriously. He died in a plane crash at 45, but his legacy was cemented forever as one of our greatest heroes. He not only had the will to join the army, but defeat multiple sicknesses and addictions, which shows us all the triumph of the human will to power.

Are you going to become what you are and ascend to a higher level?

Now it's time for the heavy artillery:

Iron Tactics.

"Your mind can be your prison, or your portal to salvation."

-Alexander Juan Antonio Cortes

SECTION TWO: IRON TACTICS

Section Two

Iron Tactics

In the first section, I prepared your mind and presented you with some new ways to look at things, and how we as humans perceive reality. We prepared our mind for the journey yet to come, and now we will look at the mental techniques and new ways to see the world. We can use these throughout life to start to gain control.

This section will require you to set aside what you think is cool, awkward, dumb, and lame. Some of the techniques I show you will seem incredibly stupid at first. You'll probably say to yourself, "I'm not doing that," or "That's some fake new age nonsense."

Let it go.

These tactics will help you gain control over your mind, and allow you to tap into strength you never thought possible. Remember, we are here to gain control over our mind. We are here to tame and focus our mind on a new level of confidence and power. You will need to set aside your preconceived notions of how "stupid" you think something is. A lot of these techniques "sound" dumb, but have been used by some of the most significant people that have ever lived. Just the fact that you are reading this book, and made it this far in, suggests that you are ready to do what's necessary to win at life.

Now let's get started acquiring the tools necessary to whip your mind into shape.

Chapter XI

Self-Talk

I used to think I was incredibly weird for talking to myself. I'm quite sure some still think I'm strange if they catch me muttering to myself. I'm sure I've been seen walking around the gym, or a place of business muttering something to myself and been thought to be nuts. I can just imagine the person seeing me do it is thinking "oh man what a psycho." That's ok though because I've learned the power of talking to myself. I have entire conversations with myself, out loud, quite often. I find that it really helps me see different sides of a debate, and allows me to clear my head. In addition, I do it to practice public speaking. I think I really came to terms with it when I read an article that showed that scientifically, we process information better when it's heard out loud[1]. Up to that point, I was always embarrassed that I did it continually. When I was a kid, as I mentioned earlier, I started doing this to cope with loneliness, by talking out stories with imaginary friends. As I got older, talking to myself never really wore off. (Well, the imaginary friend part certainly did) I've always had a very limited circle of friends, so I end up talking to myself often. Even up until l was about 35 or so, I thought it was so weird that I still did it. Now, I embrace it as a technique.

For example, when I have a presentation or training coming up, I prepare with self-talk. I take my tablet with my

---

[1] http://kiwireport.com/reading-aloud-helps-remember-information/

presentation on it, and I pace around a particular area while speaking out loud. As I hear the things I'm preparing, I edit them in real time on the tablet. Powerful phrases that are concisely focused, and understandable stay in, and vague, weak, and rambling ones go out. Hearing these phrases out loud allows me to not only practice, but to test the projection and emphasis and passion in my delivery. The more I do this, I also become more confident in my pitch, so when the time comes actually to deliver, I'm ready to go. I still get nervous every single time I do a training or presentation, but having rehearsed it in this manner really helps. Somehow, being an introvert that talks to himself has helped me immeasurably in anything public speaking related. Incidentally, a lot of professional writers will tell you to read your book aloud during the editing process. That's not an accident folks, hearing it makes a big difference in the flow and structure of the book. Some sentences will just not sound right the way you wrote it, and so reading it out loud allows you to reformat into a better delivery. So, if you think this book sucks, at the very least it sounded good to me when I read the entire thing aloud.

Another self-talk technique I do is debate with myself. I speak out loud and invent a secondary version of myself to debate both sides of an issue. Hearing a certain point come out allows me to focus on the statement, and really refine it into what I want it to be. I find I can make pretty good decisions this way, as it allows me to hear my argument, process it, and produce a counterpoint. If there's one thing I hate, it's being in one's own bubble of information as so many are these days. Between curated news feeds and TV, social media and the like, its very easy to segregate ourselves into only the groups we like and hear only the perspectives we desire. I try to avoid this and make sure I get all sides and then debate them aloud, which also prepares me to do so for real. In addition, it provides a way to check for confirmation bias and cognitive dissonance. Typically these can be very difficult to recognize in oneself, but I find that saying something aloud allows me to kind of see through my own bullshit, as it were. Check your work, as teachers used to tell me. Checking your work before you say something ignorant or making decisions based on confirmation bias.

At first, you will likely think you look stupid talking to yourself. You'll wonder what other people will think if someone sees you. It takes some time to get used to it, but once you do, it becomes extremely effectual. The reason I put this first in the tactics section, is that it is something of an enabler of the rest. You'll find the use of self-talk enhances a lot of the techniques in this section. We are going to explore more tactics regarding self-talk coming up, including a compelling technique in the next chapter: Affirmations.

Chapter XII

Affirmations

"Say unto thyself incessantly; it is in my power to keep out of my soul all wickedness, all lust, and concupiscences, all trouble and confusion."

-Marcus Aurelius, Emperor of Rome.
"Meditations."

Affirmations are another mental trick that I thought was total nonsense. For those that are unaware, affirmations are statements repeated to oneself, to affirm a particular belief. Some use them for a life goal, such as becoming say, an astronaut. Some use them to reinforce a religious conviction or a positive thing that they want to be true about themselves. They can also be used to "power up" oneself, which is generally how I use them. The premise behind them is that if you say it enough, and are doing the right things, it reinforces in your mind the idea. You've heard of the power of positive thinking; affirmations are kind of like that. By saying it to yourself, it reminds you of the goal and helps to keep you on track. It sets up a positive mental state and frame, to put you on the path for a better day. Generally, you say them every morning upon waking, and it sets the stage for a great day.

Go ahead and Google whether affirmations work or not. You will see dozens of articles that say they don't work, and dozens that say they do. On paper, they shouldn't work at all. After all, just repeating something to yourself doesn't DO anything. Some say that it can't work if it conflicts with a deeply held belief [1]. I agree with that analysis, which is why I've spent so much time in the earlier chapters trying to recalibrate your perception of life and reality. As we go forward, I hope to change your way of thinking to such a degree that you will be able to use all of these techniques in a positive manner quickly. That's why you need more than just affirmations, you need the entirety of the Iron Mind, because it is all connected, and merely one piece will be insignificant on its own.

They can also be used to power up. That's frequently how I use it. Saying a particular phrase makes one feel more powerful. You saw mine in the music chapter. I mutter it to myself, and envision myself as the conquering pharaoh or warrior, destroying all in my path. Remember that people have overwhelmingly negative thoughts most of the time. The affirmation purges these and puts you in a better mind frame. Remember too that all these tactics work together. The affirmation alone might not be enough to make a significant change, but coupled with the diet, workout, reframing, and perception changes, they will all add up to make you a powerhouse.

Here are a few examples of life goal based affirmations:

"I'm going to be a famous actor one day."

---

[1] https://www.inc.com/minda-zetlin/i-don-t-believe-in-affirmations-and-yet-they-still-work-for-me.html

"I'm going to be happy today!"

"I'm going to be stronger today than I was yesterday."

"I'll be a best selling author someday."

Remember there is a lot of self-fulfilling prophecy in any mental framework. If you believe a thing to be true, you will find ways to make it so. You can use affirmations to reinforce your mind frame and keep yourself focused. Another way to use them as I mentioned is to power up. Badass movies, books, or lyric quotes are great for this. I stole another one of mine from Mike Cernovich, who suggested in Gorilla Mindset to use the famous Apocalypse Now line: "I love the smell of napalm in the morning….smells like victory." Watch the video clip, and try that one, it works great. Remember that we want to stick to specific themes. Winning, power, conquest, strength, discipline, these are the themes we want. Anything remotely negative, weak, self-loathing, nihilistic and the like can't be options. Pick something you think is cool, that's also powerful. Remember, an affirmation can be anything that affirms what you want, or sets a positive mind frame.

My theory on why affirmations work has a lot to do with the principles behind Peale's Power of Positive Thinking, or even something like The Secret by Rhonda Byrne. That is to say, that the positivity you project helps to make things come true. Say what you want about the sort of esoteric nature of these works, but they have a lot of followers. The most significant follower I can think of at the moment is Conor McGregor, the two weight world champion in the UFC. He is a die-hard believer in the power of positive thinking, and you can even find videos online of him reading from The Secret. Now Conor is not by any means a sort of genetic freak. Sure he's talented and smart, but I would say he's no more talented than any number of UFC fighters. He does, however, have one massive advantage over most: he has an overwhelming positivity about him. I would encourage people to read his inspirational story and understand what a positive mindset has done for him.

I would say to add an affirmation or two to your daily ritual, which I will talk about in a later chapter. For now, let's keep going on tactics before we get into real-world applications.

Chapter XIII

Projection and Visualization

These techniques sound particularly odd, almost like a child's game. When you hear these terms and what they are, you think of a little girl bouncing around and acting like a princess and think "I'm not doing that!" Well, I'm here to tell you these are two of the most powerful techniques in your arsenal, and for me, they've fueled countless workout sessions. I spoke about this a bit in other chapters, and how it's related to music. This is why I believe music and the lyrics within are crucial to this technique. You can use projection techniques without music, but I believe having a setting for the projection really helps. That's why I consider picking songs based on lyrics vitally important. It allows you to choose the setting for the projection. This is why I like heavy metal. If I'm looking for a conquering warrior type of setting, there are innumerable settings like that available in metal. Hip-Hop also has a lot of scenarios that are great for this as well. Don't lock yourself into one genre though; you can find positive settings in almost any genre. I generally can't stand popular culture and music, but I do love Katy Perry's Roar or Survivor's Eye of the Tiger. You can easily find "conquering" anthems in any genre.

Projection involves inserting yourself into a fantastical setting, usually for the purposes of working out or winning at something.

I find the best ones are songs about a particular character. This is why Nile and Sabaton, two of my favorite bands, are so conducive for this purpose. They both tell very specific stories about specific individuals who did something heroic or even evil, it really doesn't matter, because we can spin the vicious into a positive mindset. Let's take the Nile song "Cast Down the Heretic." This is a song about Akhenaten, the first monotheistic ruler of Egypt. He took over, and eliminated the entire pantheon of Egyptian gods, and replaced them with one: Aten. He was eventually deposed, and the song deals with what may have happened to one who defied the priests. Its lyrics are absolutely brutal, but again, we are projecting ourselves as the punisher, not the punished.

Visualization involves creating a mental image of something to establish a positive mind frame.

I remember I first heard of the term in Arnold Schwarzenegger's BodyBuilding Encyclopedia. Back when I first read it, I thought it was just some goofy mumbo jumbo. He used to say he'd visualize a specific muscle group expanding like a massive mountain, becoming bigger than ever before. He used to say when he worked his biceps he'd envision them growing, swelling, and becoming stronger and more massive. Part of the reason this seems to work is the way the brain interprets imagery as action. [1]When I work out a particular muscle group, I like to envision the muscle being torn down, and blood thundering to the location to rebuild the muscle stronger and bigger than before. I prefer to visually imagine the muscle fibers being ripped apart by the stress of

---

[1] https://www.utcdecisionsupporttools.com/py2017/docs/01/healthy-mind/july-happy.pdf

working out and imagine the blood cells rushing to the location to slap little bits of protein onto the area, making it bigger and stronger than before. Don't just think about losing fat, envision the cells literally disintegrating as you apply effort in your cardio and workouts. Powerful visuals matter. If you are envisioning or seeing something big and powerful, the idea burrows itself into your subconscious and adds its power to your mind.

Learn to broaden and enhance your thinking. I call this 3-D Thinking. Don't just think of the particular action, learn to add a visual component and give that action dimension. I gave examples earlier here's another: Every time I have my daily herbal tea, I envision my immune system cells obliterating viruses and illnesses in my body. I'll talk more about this later in a different chapter, how to never get sick. The point is, powerful visuals work. A lot of the most effectual people that have ever walked this planet use them, and so must you learn to apply 3-D thinking to enhance the output of your thoughts. Another example comes from the world of Mixed Martial Arts. I've been watching for years, and I've always noticed something in the best fighters. They will at some point give an interview, and you will hear them say something to the effect of "I visualized the fight" or "I played the fight over in my head" and not really elaborate. The best of them, the Conor McGregor, the Georges St. Pierres, they mean that literally. They have watched footage of every minute of their opponent's fights, and have visually conceptualized themselves countering and destroying every possible move. Does it mean they win a 100% of the time? Of course not. When fists are flying anything is possible, but you can absolutely believe that it has gotten them to the highest echelon of fighting. Coupled with an indomitable will to win, these are the techniques that the masters use.

Let's take a look at another technique that can deliver intense drive:

People.

Chapter XXIV

Inventing an Enemy or Inspiration

People can be an incredible source of motivation or depression. As we talked about earlier, the toxicity audit is a technique we used to get toxic people and habits out of our lives. Now that we have rid ourselves of these destructive influences, it's time to learn how to introduce people back into your mind, but on our terms. Now that we have a much higher degree of positivity in our lives, we can find ways to add power and value back in, and people can be a wonderful source of fuel for the mind. We are going to learn two ways to do this: Inventing an Enemy and The Inspiring Hero.

Inventing an Enemy

One of the best visualization tricks you will ever find is to invent an enemy. The enemy doesn't even have to be someone you know. You can just pick someone who did something stupid most recently. It can be literally anyone who did anything to annoy you. Maybe some guy at the gym is wearing those spandex shorts and string tank top and trying to show off for the ladies. Congratulations, you're nominated to be in my projection. It could be the last significant other that cheated on you. Seriously, anyone that's ever wronged you or even slightly annoyed you can be a candidate for you to project into your obliteration or conquering song. Heck, you can also do this one without a song, just find someone to hate. I'm not big on jealousy or anything like that, but for one workout its fun to find someone to hate on for something stupid.

Inventing an enemy also carries other benefits, such as it can give you something to compete against. I like picking someone who is in better shape than me as my projection. It pushes me harder to be better and tougher than they are. Now that I'm older, I love to pick younger people as my enemy in the gym. I love taking someone who is far younger than me and trying to outwork them. At 40, I'm bigger, stronger, faster, and in better shape than the vast majority of 25-year-olds, and I fully plan to maintain that later in life. The key to this technique is to compartmentalize it. I'm sure you might be sitting there thinking, "Isn't this introducing negativity?" The answer is yes, selective negativity. We are choosing what we want to let in, and purging it immediately when it is no longer useful to us. The decisions we are making now are conscious. We removed the toxic influencers, then bring them back temporarily to power our workouts, on our terms.

Kobe Bryant was one of the foremost masters of this technique. He could manufacture out of thin air an unstoppable will to win, just based on a perceived slight by someone. During his feud with Shaquille O'Neal, he continually used the statements in the media by Shaq to fuel himself. Shaq infamously told Kobe to "Eat his ass" after winning title number four, and Kobe used that to drive himself to another level and to eventually surmount Shaq at five titles. Do not underestimate how powerful this technique is, but learn to set it aside when necessary so as not to consume your life. Unless you are in pursuit of world titles, then by all means, go full Kobe Bryant. The ability to manufacture this type of intensity is potent, so I would recommend doing this as a temporary one off in the gym, not a lifelong feud unless you are an outlier like Kobe who is considered one of the greatest of all time.

Inventing an enemy is great, but there's an inverse too.

The Inspiring Hero

This is one of my favorites. I love finding someone who is working out and overcoming extreme odds that are far worse than my own. Back in my more hardcore lifting days, I had a couple of people that went to the gym that fueled me, and they never even knew it. One lady there, who I assumed was in her early 30s, was in ridiculous shape. Full six pack; the whole deal. I went to the gym with her and worked out in her vicinity for years, and I found out years later, she was 45 and has three kids. The person in the best shape there had three freaking kids, a marriage, and a job. Any excuse I could make pales in comparison to her example. Another of my favorites is the "Super Ripped Old Guy." Every gym has at least one of these. There's always some old guy in his 60s or 70s who is just in ridiculous shape. I love those guys. Talk about amazing motivators, just seeing guys like that fired me up. Look for people like that in your gym, or even life, and use that to fuel you. Use it to eliminate excuses. If that girl who is 40 years old and has three kids can have a badass physique, then what the hell is my excuse?

I used to be super into Pro Wrestling. I loved the personalities involved because it was basically soap operas for guys. One of my favorite wrestlers in the 90s and early 2000s was HHH, or Hunter Hearst Helmsley, real name Jean-Paul Levesque. He was about my same height 6'3", and had the same long blond hair I had, but he was mega buff. He was one of my early inspirations because of the height and hair; he was an obvious avatar to project myself onto. He looked and acted like I wanted to look and act. This was right around the time I started working out, so I was on the right path, but I was nowhere near as built as he was, nor was I anywhere near as confident or funny. HHH was wrestling one night and completely tore the Quadricep muscle off the bone in his leg. He finished out the match like the tough bastard he is, but he was definitely really hurt. He was out for months rehabbing and having surgery to correct the injury, and we couldn't wait for him to come back. Finally, we got word he was going to show up on RAW, the WWE's flagship show on a Monday night.

His music hit and he came out, and the crowd predictably erupted. After being gone eight months to a massive, devastating injury, he came out. My friend and I that were watching this spectacle looked at each other and said the same thing:

"How is this guy so fucking massive?"

It was true. He was an absolute monster. Bigger and more built than when he left. In writing this, I actually watched it again on YouTube and relived it a bit. He was absolutely bigger, stronger, and better than when he left. This event was fuel for a lot of workouts for me. Now, I get it, I'm sure he was on steroids or something, but that isn't the point. The point was that he suffered a devastating injury and came back better than he was before. Generally, I'm against having "heroes," but I definitely recommend inspirations. It can be a person, or an event, whatever you need to jack you up to another level. Beyond creating an enemy or finding inspiration, the question then becomes:

Can you be that inspiration for someone else? Can you change someone's life just from them observing you? That becomes the ultimate challenge. Will a child walk up to you and say "I want to be like you one day." You can't inspire others without first mastering yourself. We now have the basics down, so let's get a little deeper. It's time to manipulate your perceptions of life and reality itself. We've already touched on some of this, but now its time to forge ahead.

Chapter XXV

Dominating the Frame Game

I'm going to introduce you to one of the most useful tactics you will ever come across: Reframing.

First, let's establish what it means to "frame" something. Framing is a way of structuring or presenting a problem or an issue. Framing involves explaining and describing the context of the obstacle to gain the most support from your audience. Your audience is key to framing. The way a problem is posed or framed should reflect the attitudes and beliefs of your audience[1].

Now, as you see in that definition, framing is largely defined as audience-based. So for example, if you are talking to an audience of Mac users, it doesn't help to "frame" the thing you are talking about in the context of a Windows function. It is also a debate tactic. If the opposition brings up a difficult point, a masterful debater will "reframe" the question into a position that is more conversant with the views of the audience. In other words, reframing is generally used as a way to direct the conversation in the way you would like it to go. Here's an example. Let's say you have an immigration policy debate. You can watch these on any cable news channel at all hours of the day.

---

[1] https://masscommtheory.com/theory-overviews/framing-theory/

1. Conservative stresses the need for limited immigration.
2. Democrat reframes to a story of an individual immigrant that has been hurt by the policy, playing the empathy card to the audience.
3. Conservative reframes into illegal immigrant violence, telling a story of a family that lost a child to illegal immigrant violence.

In that story, and in all debates, the side that holds their respective frame in the most effective manner, is likely perceived by the audience to be the winner. Reframing becomes necessary when the opposition puts up a strong enough point that you can't counter without losing support. This is an incredibly strong technique regarding any negotiation or persuasion, which are used consistently throughout life.

There is another powerful way to use reframing: For yourself.

Now, knowing that framing is audience-based, what happens if YOU are the audience? I do not mean that you are the audience of another speaker, I mean that you are the only audience, with your inner monologue as the speaker. I talked a bit about reframing earlier in the chapter on music. I used a Slayer song as an example. Reframing works on almost anything negative. Learning to reframe in seconds anything negative is an essential skill to building the Iron Mind. Reframing is taking something that appears to be one thing, and flipping it into another thing very quickly in your head. For example, let's take a real-life scenario of someone making you angry at work. The first step is something negative happens that really pisses you off. As soon as the event is over, you're likely to start thinking about how much you hate that person, and how much you hate your job and want to quit. Instead, as soon as you recognize that happening, reframe the thought immediately into something empowering, such as: "I'm getting so good at handling that type of thing," or "Man, when I get that promotion I'm not going to have to handle that type of thing as much." Keep in mind doing this also purges the actual event from your memory, because you are occupying your mind with setting up the new frame.

Learning to change the frame is not only incredibly useful when dealing with other people, but it is also incredibly useful on yourself to maintain positivity. Every once in awhile something will happen that makes me really mad. I'll be simmering, and my breathing becomes ragged and harsh. There was a time when I would explode in rage and say something mean to someone, or get really nasty. Now, I've learned as quickly as that feeling hits, to change the frame instantly. Here's an example:

One morning I woke up to a puddle on my kitchen floor. I immediately thought to myself "Oh shit I don't know a damn thing about plumbing" and started to get angry over the situation, since I had things planned for that morning. I felt myself developing anger and thought to myself, "You know what? I don't know jack shit about plumbing, and I'm 40 years old. Now will be a great time to learn a few new things, I'll need this skill again later." So, I made a project out of it. Instead of getting angry, I turned the frame around into a learning frame that will benefit me down the road, because now I know a considerable amount more about faucets and some plumbing.

Learning to maintain a powerful frame, and reframing weak ones really helps to prevent stress from developing in the first place.

Play the frame game correctly, and it will enable incredible mental control, as well as saving you a tremendous amount of stress. Also, it will make negotiating or any sales much smoother. It takes a lot of practice, but it is one of the most valuable skills you can have.

> *"If you are distressed by anything external, the pain is not due to the thing itself, but to your estimate of it; and this you have the power to revoke at any moment."*
>
> — *Marcus Aurelius, Emperor of Rome, Meditations*

Chapter XXVI

The Power of Shame

"I have only a second-rate brain, but I think I have a capacity for action."

-Theodore Roosevelt

Ed Latimore, former pro boxer, and current mindset expert wrote a book called Not Caring What Other People Think is a Superpower. This is 100% iron mind truth. There is very little in life that can make a greater difference than being able to eliminate shame. One of my former bosses said about me once: "I like Steve because he's an action guy, he just does things." Incidentally, this was a boss I clashed with A LOT. But we eventually got along, because he saw me as someone who didn't play around. If he asked us to do something, I did it immediately and usually first. Or vocally told him why I wasn't going to do it and we would then have an animated discussion. Either way, both require a virtual elimination of the thing known as shame. One of my best friends said something similar about me, but he said it this way: "Man I wish I could be more like Steve he just doesn't give a fuck." So I've heard the same thing from numerous people, and it isn't about not giving a fuck. It's about the complete elimination of shame. As Ed Latimore says in his book, it really is a superpower not to care what other people think.

I used to be wracked with the insecurity of what people thought about me. Whether it was the girl in my class I had a crush on, the group of popular kids in high school that I wanted to be like, or the bodybuilder I worked out next to that gave me a case of body dysmorphia. No matter what or who it was, I was in a constant state of worry about what people thought about me. Think about your life. Think about the sheer amount of people we want to impress or have positive thoughts about us. There are easily more than a dozen people in our orbit at any given time we are trying to impress. Now imagine how you would execute if you didn't care at all what they thought. Would you just walk right up to that girl and ask her out? Would you immediately ask for a promotion or raise? My guess is that the fear of shame for a lot of people, as it used to be for me, is a driving force in their life.

I will tell you a story about my lack of shame. There was a girl I worked with for many years; I will call her Jessica. I had a crush on this girl like you can't believe. There was only one problem: The entire time I knew her she had a boyfriend that she was fiercely loyal to. Now, I see how a lot of modern men operate; they befriend a girl under the guise of "friendship" then work behind the scenes to undermine their current relationship in the hopes that they will "see the light" and realize their undying affection for the friend that's been there all this time. I always found that to be a slimy, underhanded thing to do. I knew her boyfriend wasn't good enough for her, but I didn't actively work to undermine him, she had to come to that realization herself. Year after year passed. I told myself whenever I was single that if Jessica EVER became available I'd go for it. Now, make no mistake, this wasn't an obsession. I still dated plenty of other people, so it's not as if I wasted years waiting. After about four years, we were talking one day, and she said the magic words: "I broke up with him."

Immediately, without hesitation, I said, "Good now you can date me," with a smirk. She thought I was joking, but I said, "Well, once you are over the breakup, I want the first date." For weeks I pursued her, and guess what?

I never got a date.

The girl I wanted for years rejected me. Total and complete failure. So why do I tell this story now? First and foremost: I know, beyond a shadow of a doubt that I did everything I could. I left nothing on the table in pursuit of Jessica. I will not sit here 20 years from now and wonder what could have been if I had just had the balls to say something when I had the chance. I've talked out how I don't do regret before. Part of not having regret is not leaving things on the table you'll think about down the road. I know, unequivocally, that I gave it my best shot with Jessica and it didn't pan out. Secondly, this story illustrates my total lack of shame. The minute I had the opportunity, I seized it. I didn't win, but at least I know the result and don't have to sit here and wonder what could have been. This is another great life lesson we can get from Star Wars. Yoda said in the Last Jedi:

> *"The Greatest teacher, failure is."*
>
> *-Yoda*

Imagine my life 20 years from now if I had been worried about shame. I would always have this mythological image of Jessica in my head that I built up. I'd be envisioning this wonderful life we could have had if I had just gone for it. This is part of not living in the past and going for the future at all times. We are going to talk about this in the next chapter.

Chapter XXVII

Shaping Your Reality

Steve Jobs famously had something that experts called a "Reality Distortion Field." What they meant by that was that Steve Jobs had extraordinary persuasion technique that was so good he could convince the entire world what he believed to be true. Why do I bring Steve Job's sales skills into a book about self-improvement? Because you need to be good at creating the reality around you. You can, through your actions, set the way that the world unfolds around you, and actually think yourself into a new reality. As you gain the Iron Mind, you can then use it to warp reality itself around you.

One thing I've never given two shits about is regret. I spend virtually zero time screwing around in the past. We all have things we've done in the past that we really wish we could have back. I'm here to tell you that you have to stop that shit right now. Regret is bullshit. You can't ever have it back, so all you can do is:

Make the past not matter.

"When is the best time to plant a tree? 20 years ago."

"When is the second best time? Right now."

I'm telling you right now, that the past and the present don't matter. What we want to do is describe the future by ignoring the past and present. How things were and are don't mean shit. Sure, every once in awhile you want to reflect back on the past, but only in service of the future. Use the lessons learned in the past to influence positive outcomes in the future. One of the best quotes on this comes from one of the more evil fictional characters: Kylo Ren in Star Wars. He says: "Let the past die. Kill it if you have to. It's the only way to become what you were meant to be." So, I'm not going to advocate killing your parents as he did, but there is a ton of truth in that line. Being tethered to the past will never allow you to move forward and become the best version of yourself. In the case of moving forward with your life, history is the enemy. Let me repeat. It is fine to learn lessons from history, but understand that as it relates to advancing your life, history becomes the enemy. Too many people are obsessed with how something happened in the past, with a completely different set of conditions and people. Things are never the same from one instance to the next. Do not let history dictate your future. Fictional character quotes are great, but let's look at some real-life examples. Here's one, and it's from possibly the best reality shaper any of us have ever seen.

Donald Trump.

I've talked about Trump a lot in this book. Whether you like him or not, he a virtual gold mine of lessons to be learned. Even if you hate Trump, if you aren't learning from him, you are doing it all wrong. Currently, in the first year of his presidency, people have called him everything from imbecile to clown to Hitler. Maybe so. Maybe he is a total moron. So let's take an objective look at what this moron has accomplished:
1. President of the United States.
2. Multi-Billionaire.

3. Multiple Time Bestselling Author.
4. World Famous Celebrity.
5. Tons of great kids and grandkids that all love him.
6. Tight Family.
7. Tons of massive companies and buildings.

So, somehow half the country still thinks this guy slipped on a banana peel and just lucked up into all this success. I've explained other elements of Trump in other areas, but now I'm going to touch on maybe his greatest ability: Reality shaping. During the campaign, Trump made immigration a top priority. He came out harder than anyone, talked about a massive wall, deportation forces, the whole nine yards. He positioned himself as the toughest imaginable on illegal immigration. On his inauguration, illegal immigration plummeted. Within a month it was down over 70% without a single piece of legislation. Watch how Trump talks, he is always doing one thing:

Describing the Future.

He is relentless in the way he is constantly describing the way things are going to be. Whether it's trade, immigration, or the economy, he is absolutely relentless in his positive rhetoric. The immigration issue I mentioned earlier is a prime example because he literally created the future just by saying it. By positioning himself as the toughest guy that ever lived on immigration, he immediately de-incentivized anyone to come here illegally, because they understood he would be the biggest illegal immigration badass of all time. Through his rhetoric alone, he created a future in which we have way less illegal immigration. Now take the economy. A lot of people just assume the economy is some abstract jobs plus supply algorithm. Here's what a huge percentage of the economy is: Optimism. The minute Trump took office, the economy exploded. Consumer and investor confidence erupted. The stock market hit an all-time high. Almost 4.5 trillion in new wealth created, without a single piece of legislation. Trump managed to talk the economy into a boom. You see, the economy and investments are mainly a self-fulfilling prophecy. If people THINK the economy is going to be good, then they invest and hire. Trump sold them on the idea that America was going to be awesome again, that regulations were going to go away, and there would be massive tax cuts. So in other words, Trump literally spoke a new reality into existence.

This isn't just for multi-billionaires. You can talk yourself into a positive future. This is what Norman Vincent Peale (A Trump influencer) talks about in The Power of Positive Thinking.

> *"Formulate and stamp indelibly on your mind a mental picture of yourself succeeding. Hold this picture tenaciously and never let it fade. Your mind will seek to develop the picture, never let obstacles enter your mind."*
>
> *-Norman Vincent Peale*

Here's another thing Trump does that applies to what we are talking about. He almost never talks about the past. Ever notice that? He doesn't allow himself to be roped into anything negative regarding his past. If an interviewer asks him about some bankruptcy he had 15 years ago, he will ALWAYS redirect into talk of how successful he's been and how awesome he's going to be moving forward. This is not an accident, and it's not him trying to hide something. It's him constantly projecting a winning aura. It's him shifting reality from something bad into overall how awesome he is, but importantly how awesome things are going to be. He rides this formula over and over. Watch any interview he's ever done, and you can watch him spin a positive future in real time. Some people call that lying or being a con man. I call it smart. He is talking the future into developing the way he wants it to, and discussing something that happened in the past isn't helping him do that, so he redirects immediately. The only piece of information he needs from the past is that he's been successful overall. A failure here and there doesn't matter to him; he only sees how things have developed overall.

I've watched hundreds of people try to lose weight. Between my actual training in real life, and shows on TV like the Biggest Loser, I've seen people struggle and fail, and struggle and succeed. The difference, 90%+ of the time is whether or not they can overcome mental blocks from their past. If you really sit down and get intimate with someone trying to lose weight, there is almost always a mental block from the past that is stopping them. Whether it's their relationship with their parents, or sense of self-worth from bullying, or support from a significant other, you can guarantee almost 100% of the time that the past is holding someone back. That's why I tell you that learning to destroy the past is beyond critical. If your sense of self is tethered to things or people from the past, you are going to have a very difficult time moving forward positively.

Kill the past. Learn to envision the future instead.

> *"The Best Way To Predict The Future Is To Create It."*
>
> *-Abraham Lincoln*

Here's another example: I talk myself into good workouts. Say I go to the gym and I have a great workout. When I'm walking out of the gym, thoroughly spent, having destroyed whichever body part was on the menu that day, I start to envision how I'm going to crush the next one. I'll think something to the effect of "God I can't wait to get back here the next time, I'm going to fucking annihilate this next one." Basically, I'm setting myself up to be in a killer mind frame for the next workout. Over the course of the next day or so, I'll build it up in my mind. I'll just constantly repeat how I'm going to crush this next workout and how I can't wait for it. By the time the actual workout arrives, I'm so geared up it's almost impossible not to have a great workout.

Imagine yourself into a better future. Don't allow yourself to project failure.

Chapter XVIII

The Story of Future You

The act of reading this book has actively changed who you will be in the future. You are at a pivotal moment. The You that exists today is now dead. Future You will either be better or worse ten years or even ten days from now. Everyone has pivotal moments in their life. Events that shape how the future develops. I've always been fascinated by how the events of one's life unfold due to the smallest decision made, in some cases, decades earlier. Maybe you left your house 1 minute late, and because of that 1 minute, you got in a car accident that changed the trajectory of your life. For anyone into sci-fi, you'll recognize the term "Butterfly Effect." Basically the gist of it is is that one tiny change ripples forward into massive changes over time. Every choice we make creates a ripple in time, affecting us irrevocably down the line. Who you will be 20 years from now can be fundamentally changed by a decision you make today.

> *"We all make choices, but in the end our choices make us."*
>
> *Andrew Ryan - Bioshock*

The events that have happened to you in your life cannot be changed. I can't know the depths of suffering that's far beyond my own that some of you may have experienced. What can be changed is how you respond to them. I know people that even decades later, still have not been able to reconcile past events. The lover that jilted them, the accident that injured them continues to haunt them and play havoc in their lives. Remember that you are writing your own story every day. Every day that goes by that you are dwelling on past events is ensuring that your narrative doesn't have a happy ending. I know people that obsess over lovers, or upbringing and just the past in general. As I mentioned earlier, the past holds back so many people, so I'm here to present a new tactic for moving forward and writing your own story.

The Story of Future You.

I've introduced several concepts such as reframing, affirmations, and projecting. The Story of Future You requires them all. I've found when getting people to let go of the past and focus on the future, the most useful tool is…

Yourself.

More precisely, the version of yourself that you want to be. Envision your life as it's played out up until now. Think of the events that have shaped who you have become. Maybe a lost love, a severe accident, bullying, a fight. Think about a specific situation, and think about how you developed over the years based on that one event. Did growing up religious turn you against religion in your later years? Did being wronged by a significant other turn you against all members of that gender for a time? The first part of this exercise is you have to put down, on paper, a one sentence line.

What kind of person do I want to be in the future?

Then you have to answer the following question:

How does what I'm doing now make that possible?

In the previous chapter, I talked about killing the past to move forward into a better future for yourself. This is how you do it. Instead of focusing on the past, focus on the person that matters:

Future You.

Is what I'm doing right now, or what I'm focused on right now, good for Future Me? As you sit here reading this book, you are currently writing your own story. As I sit here and write these words, I know Future Me is thrilled that I'm writing them, and not sitting in the other room playing games or watching TV. Future Me approves of this action I'm taking right now. So if you are, for example, pining over how much a lover wronged you, then you are ensuring at this moment in time, that your story has an unhappy ending. Let me tell you a story, it's about a girl named Lucy. Lucy fell in love with a man, and her heart was full of joy. He disappeared one day, only to re-emerge two weeks later, engaged to a non-Lucy woman. Her heart was shattered. She was the other woman. Lucy sunk into the depths of depression, asking why, pouring her heart out in her journals. She plotted to get revenge, to ruin his life for having the temerity to ruin hers.

Let's take a look at Lucy. Let's say she schemes for weeks or months to get revenge on him for what he did. Let's even grant that she somehow does get revenge, and gets away with it. How does this improve Lucy's story? It makes a magnificent novel for someone else to read, but how is this story improving the ending for Lucy herself? She will have wasted months, if not years in pursuit of reconciling a past that can't ever be changed. Imagine the happiness Lucy could have made for herself if she redirected all that energy into Future Lucy. The only way Lucy's story beats his is if she is happier than he is. His destruction is missing out on her, and the person she becomes. If Lucy decides she wants Future Lucy to be happy, kind, and forgiving, then she must pursue that end.

In addition, another tool you can use is the reverse of what I've been talking about: Future Hell. I spoke about envisioning precisely the type of person you want to be ten years from now, but there's a reversal of that as well. Envisioning a worst-case outcome ten years from now, and envisioning the types of decisions you'd have to make to make that a reality. Let's say you envision that you are a homeless person living under a bridge ten years from now. How many decisions would you have to make to end up like that? Maybe you kept around a toxic person too long, or you became an alcoholic, whatever the case, get specific. If you are about to have a whiskey, get drunk and pass out on the couch, think really hard about how that decision rolls forward through time and eventually brings you to a catastrophic point.

You do have a choice, to be the person you want to be, and you had better make the right one.

Future You is counting on it.

Chapter XIX

Iron Attitude

There's a tremendous amount of mental tricks and techniques we can use to help build the Iron Mind. However, at some point, we need to adjust our attitude. How we carry ourselves and deal with other people and interpersonal relationships in the real world makes a huge difference in our mind frame.

Dress code Matters.

Even something as simple as the way we dress can have a massive impact on our lives. When I was a younger man, I absolutely hated NFL Hall of Famer Deion Sanders. For those that don't know, he was loud, flamboyant, and highly skilled. At the time, I was very bashful, so I saw a brash, confident man and just didn't like the fact that he was so outspoken. He was everything I was not: confident, brash, successful, and I disliked him for it. Looking back, he was right about a lot of things, and instinctively did a lot of the things I talk about in this book. He had a quote that turned out to be incredibly accurate:

> *"Look good, feel good. Feel good, play good.*
> *Play good; they pay good."*

> *Deion Sanders*

Sounds simple, but that's why it's brilliant. A lot of the way you carry yourself and act ends up being a self-fulfilling prophecy because you are literally faking your way into making yourself actually better. Deion understood that if he "felt" good by dressing nice, it would positively impact his play. So, in crafting our confident, powerful mind, we have to start with the basics:

Dressing well absolutely influences mind frame.

This is one it took me decades to get. I used to hate any sort of fashion, hell in a lot of ways I still do. I literally owned probably 50 black heavy metal shirts, and a few pairs of jeans. That's it. Every piece of clothing I had was ill-fitting, ultra basic everyday garb. I don't want to dress up, I swear to god. I hate all the preparation and shopping and all that nonsense, I really do. However, when I put the time in and I know damn well I look awesome, I have to admit its the right choice. Dressing well gives you a psychological edge and confidence looking like crap doesn't. When you look good, your mindset shifts to a more positive place and even your posture almost immediately gets better. Now, I'm not suggesting you have to get all dressed up to go to Walmart or anything, but never, ever look like a slob. Get clothes that actually fit, not that are all baggy and loose fitting. Another thing I recommend is to always get dressed. Even if you are just going to hang around the house all day, still get dressed. It puts you in the mindset to work, or get moving around, as opposed to laying around in your underwear.

God, I used to hate people that dressed up all the time. I'd think to myself, what a waste of time and money, while I'd spend a zillion dollars on some game or another trivial hobby. In an earlier chapter, I told you that I could tell a tremendous amount about someone just by looking at their car or how messy their house is. Well, I've got news for you, it's the same on your attire. Think of this, if you had to ask a question, and two people were standing there, and one was a slob, and one was sharp, in whose answer would you be more confident? Now look, no one is saying you need to run out and buy a Rolex you can't afford. Looking good is highly subjective anyway, and we don't want to break the bank to do it. You can dress nicely without spending a zillion dollars. Get things that match, are decent quality, and fit correctly and that's half the battle. The point is to put in the effort, and you'll feel good after, guaranteed.

Posture is critical.

This is another big area modern people seem to think isn't a priority. Just about everyone seems to have garbage posture from staring at their phones all day like a bunch of drones, or slouching in their seat as they binge-watch their 13th episode of some shitty Netflix series in a row, or just walking around like the hunchback of Notre Dame. Maybe you sit in a cubicle at a desk staring at a computer screen all day. This area has to be addressed. Besides the fact that ergonomics matter to health, having shitty posture actually makes you feel worse. I will put it this way, I don't recall ever seeing someone in charge, who really had their shit together, who didn't have confident posture. Ever notice how every CEO just happens to have that same confident swagger? Man or woman doesn't matter, people who are winners carry themselves as such. They don't slink around with drooped shoulders and hung heads. They walk like they own the place. Not only that, it's not only CEOs that you see that carry themselves that way.

Sometimes you'll know someone in a very low-level position that's just really confident about what they are doing.

Posture makes a big difference to how we feel physically, but mentally as well. Make a concerted effort to hold your head high. Make sure your shoulders don't droop and walk like you know what the hell you are doing. All of these things I tell you individually can make a difference, but all added together can make a massive difference in your mind frame. Dressing great and having good posture alone is nice, but add both, and you have a real winner.

Get your ass up.

Seriously, this is a big one of mine. I walk everywhere. I park as far away as I can from entrances. I never take escalators. Always take the stairs. Let me just say; I hate doing cardio at the gym. Cannot stand it. I would much rather get my cardio at the park, or throughout the day. I have one rule for any traversal I do on my feet:

Make it difficult.

Everywhere I have to walk; I find the steepest incline. Any opportunity I have to take stairs instead of an elevator. Parking further away not only keeps my car doors from getting dented from a bunch of assholes parking too close to me, but it also gets in some steps.

> *"I wish to preach not the doctrine of ignoble ease, but the doctrine of the strenuous life."*
>
> -Theodore Roosevelt

Get a dog.

Walking the dog is my favorite. First, dogs need to explore and get exercise. I feel so guilty if I don't walk him enough. He gets me out in the cold and hot weather and motivates me to pick up my pace. If you don't have a dog, get one. Besides the unconditional love and amazing ability to pick you up, they are magnificent exercise motivators. He always wants his walk, and he wants nothing more than to have one with his daddy. Sometimes you wake up and its absurdly cold, so you might think of making an excuse to not go to the gym, or whatever, but there he is looking out the window wanting to go for a walk. He guilt trips me into being stronger and not skipping walks or gym time. Dogs are great motivators because they are single-minded. It's forward and following the nose no matter what. Every day and every interaction is new to them. Even if you left the house for 30 seconds, they act like they haven't seen you for a month. You will never get that level of love even from family. They forgive instantly and love unconditionally. There is no being that can match the dog. All you cat people can go on all you want about how cats are more independent and think for themselves, but it doesn't matter because dogs are objectively better. Think of this, what other animal has done more in service to humanity and saved more lives than dogs? Military, Law Enforcement, Rescue, dogs are the greatest servants of humanity ever to exist.

Get one, and one day you'll understand.

Never apologize.

This sounds really counter-intuitive. Why would you not apologize when you've been wrong? First off, this only works if you have supreme confidence in yourself and what you are doing. It is guaranteed in some cases to generate conflict because you will be standing up for positions you've taken or things that you've done that might not be popular. Here's the key whether or not to apologize.

Did someone get hurt because of an objectively incorrect decision you made?

That's about it. Note that I also added the word objectively in there. Keep in mind a lot what I've talked about in this book is that facts don't matter as much as you think they do. Someone might think it's a "fact" that you made an incorrect decision. That is the opposite of a fact, that's likely an interpretation. I got into a massive fight with a boss once because I told him that our purchaser sucks because we didn't have enough of a certain product. Here's how that conversation went:

Me: "Hey Man we have got to get some of X, Y, and Z, what the fuck is Ms. Purchaser doing up there?"

Boss: "Oh she did everything she could we couldn't get any of those because the company was out of funds for the year."

Me: "Damn she's awful, they need to find someone new, we never have X, Y, and Z and we lose massive business because of it."

Boss: "No they just didn't have the money, there's nothing you can do in a situation like that."

Me: "Uh yeah there is. Well, there was at least.."

Boss: "No there isn't. They didn't have money. That's a fact. You can't argue with a fact."

Me: "Sure I can. They had money at one point. She just didn't convince them to invest it in our products."

So there's an example. Facts are largely interpretations. Was he absolutely correct? Yes, he was. But so was I. During the early stages of Trump's Presidency, his advisor Kellyanne Conway got blasted for using a term called alternative facts. Everyone trashed her to no end saying things like: "There's no such thing as alternative facts, you are just lying." I have got news for all of those people. Alternative facts are definitely real. You might be able to come up with ten facts as to why Trump sucks, and I can come up with 20 alternative facts as to why he doesn't. Remember that we interpret everything through our own worldview, and almost nothing other than decisions with no emotional component are valid objective facts. An actual fact is something that has no emotional component, such as the following:

This product is 20 dollars.

If I walk in front of a speeding bus, I will likely die.

My car has an engine.

My dog has a tail.

Those are objective facts because they have no emotional component to them. Even that first example might not be an objective fact if the prices are negotiable.

So how does this all tie into not saying you're sorry? You should never apologize when you believe you are right. Make your case. Apologizing immediately puts you at the mercy of the other person, who may or may not accept your apology. It shows weakness, and a willingness to cave on something you didn't believe in the first place. I've gotten into massive confrontations with multiple bosses over the years because I didn't back down on things I believed. Also, I've had virtually all of them tell me they loved the fact that I was the only one willing to take a stand. You see, bosses are going to get a lot, certainly the majority, telling them what they want to hear. In most cases, it will be extremely rare for them to have someone that stands up to them and fights for something. If you have ever run anything, then you know its very difficult to get good ideas from people, because they are always trying to say what they think you want to hear. By standing your ground on things you believe in, you immediately become an outlier. They may fire back and get fierce with you, but sometimes you have to fire back. Apologizing just because you think it's what you are supposed to do is the wrong move. It is almost always the right move to double down, as long as you have the confidence that you've put the proper thought into it. If I believe I'm right, I will go to my grave fighting for it, and my bosses have massively respected that fact.

No one respects a weenie. Backing down for the sake of backing down is almost always a horrible idea, both at work and in relationships. Here's another story that illustrates this. I had a slacker boss once a long time ago. Long story short, he was fired and replaced. The new guy had a reputation for being a hardass. He blasted us all on the first conference call and had us all quaking in our boots that we might be fired next since we were an underperforming region. I had never met him before, and I heard he was going to be in my area soon. He finally showed up, and the first thing he did was blast me over my shirt. I was wearing a nice business casual shirt, not the company shirt. I had been with the company for four years and been told explicitly that I could wear a business shirt. He showed up and lit into me over my shirt.

"Why the Hell are you wearing that shirt?"

"(Confused) What do you mean?"

"That isn't the company shirt Steve."

"I was told I could wear business casual."

"You were told wrong, why the hell are you wearing it?"

"Hey look, I've been here for four years and been given express permission to wear this type of thing."

"Well don't do it again."

"No problem."

Do not get in the habit of apologizing for stuff that isn't your fault. It would have been easy to apologize for the shirt and not have a confrontation. Part of me thinks he was picking stuff on all of us to test us and see how we'd respond. I actually fought a lot with that boss, and he told me much later that I was one of his favorites because I wasn't a yes man. I always gave feedback and stuck to my guns on my beliefs. You will earn a higher degree of respect. No one, and I mean no one, likes a doormat. When your significant other is pressing you, or your boss is all over you, the first instinct is to cave. Learn to battle respectfully. You don't have to tell them to go to hell, but being a perpetual apologizer isn't going to get you anywhere either, especially not in the long run.

Everyone hates Passive Aggressiveness.

Everyone. Seriously. If you are a passive aggressive person, no one likes you. Not only that, they don't even respect you. I know people who go through their job or life, utterly oblivious to the fact that no one around them actually likes them, save a small group of friends that are just giving them a pass. Also, most people don't even recognize they are doing something that is really annoying to everyone else. If you are passive aggressive, then you are perceived as weak. You are regarded as someone too weak to say what they think up front, which automatically reduces your perceived value. Passive aggressive actions can include:

1. Purposefully doing a mediocre job to get back at a boss.
2. Latent Hostility in Communication style.
3. Avoiding conflict at all cost, even when you are right.
4. Always playing the perpetual victim.
5. Overuse of sarcasm to denigrate others.
6. Always playing on the guilt of others.

If you are perpetuating any of these behaviors, it's time for a re-education, because you are going nowhere fast. Let me put it to you this way. The opposite, which I call Active Aggressive, can be perceived as being rude, loud, and confrontational. However, there is also a massive upside, because it also has the side effect of appearing passionate and caring. Someone who is brash and active aggressive will, at the very least, be respected for giving a shit. Passive aggressive gets zero respect from anyone. The person who is bold and brash will always be perceived as higher value. If you want an marvelous example of one vs. the other, all you have to do is watch Jeb Bush vs. Donald Trump in the Republican Primaries. Trump destroyed Bush for a variety of reasons, persuasion technique, strength projection, etc., but one big reason is that Bush was ridiculously passive-aggressive, which is a big reason he was crushed so easily. In their debates, Trump looked like an asshole, but he also seemed like the strong one. He looked like he gave a shit. And now he's the President. If you take anything away from this, it's do not be like Jeb Bush. You don't have to be as brash and in your face as Trump either but find that middle ground.

At all costs, DO NOT BE PASSIVE AGGRESSIVE. It will sabotage your career, personal life, everything. Go out of your way to say what you think, and stand up for yourself. It will pay dividends as your value elevates in the eyes of everyone around you, and will solve problems you didn't even know you had. So here's what I propose:

Not Passive Aggressive.

Not Active Aggressive.

Active Assertive.

This is the sweet spot of where you want to be, and to what this entire chapter has been building. This is the style that communicates clearly, powerfully, and confidently, without being an asshole. You are no one's doormat, and always follow through with what you say you will do. You make well thought out, ambitious decisions, without undercutting people unnecessarily. You dress well, walk with confident posture, and become well respected and admired amongst your peers and leaders.

That is the goal, now let's take a look at how this attitude impacts your ego.

Chapter XX

The Humility Fetish

"I knew I was a winner back in the late sixties. I knew I was destined for great things. People will say that kind of thinking is totally immodest. I agree. Modesty is not a word that applies to me in any way - I hope it never will.

-Arnold Schwarzenegger

We have fetishized humility these days. Watching people fall all over themselves not to take credit for absolutely anything has become an amusing spectator sport for me. I love watching post-game interviews with athletes to see how fast they can call something a "team effort" or "great coaching" or any other miscellaneous platitudes. Interviews have now become an exercise in tedium because no one wants to be called a narcissist or arrogant. Everyone wants to extol the virtues of the "team" as much as they possibly can, to the point of making interviews pointless. Here's an example of mine based on a former coworker I will call Bill:

Bill was one of the absolute best at his job I ever worked with. No one and I mean no one could compete with him when he was at his best, and that includes me. I was damn good at what I did, but it always frustrated me that I couldn't beat Bill. Bill got every result right, I might top him at one thing, but he'd surpass me in 6 other metrics. That's how it worked. He was just amazing at this job we both had. However, Bill had one crippling flaw. He had a humility fetish. He refused to take any credit for anything. This guy could dominate the entire group, and he'd always redirect any praise to the team or his coworkers. Maybe his family, but it was always something. This was problematic for several reasons. One, he never got promoted. He did such a good job convincing people how awesome everyone else was, that he made his actual talent and results not seem as important. In other words, he made himself appear expendable. Two, it hurt the rest of us because we never could get his tactics down. Instead of recognizing how awesome he was and sharing it with the rest of us, he put the praise on others, which didn't help the rest of the team in the least. So in reality, his humility actually hurt the rest of the team because we never learned much from him.

So what do I mean by fetishizing humility? This is a concept I learned from a recent Scott Adams talk, where he described it as people rushing to project their virtue, or virtue signaling as I like to call it. We've gotten to the point in society now where taking any credit at all makes you a malignant narcissist, or to mean that you are full of yourself. Being optimistic or thinking positively about yourself has actually become demonized. I'd make the argument that this humility fetish has become more prominent in the years since socialism has become trendy, because in the socialist utopia that a lot of leftists want, individualism is erased, and it's all a collective, like a bunch of Borg drones from Star Trek. No one is better than anyone else; no one is special, we all just act as a collective. The modern leftist wants to permanently erase any meritocracy from the planet, and make everything a collectivist state. There's a zillion reasons why that will never work, but there is one huge overriding one:

Human Nature.

There are going to be people that are outliers, which are smarter, faster, stronger, but most of all above all else: More determined. There are going to be successful people, and not all of them are going to be smarter than you. Most of the time, it was a matter of determination and putting themselves in position to get lucky. You need to believe in your skills. Having a humility fetish I'd argue is actually harmful, you need to embrace your narcissism. Give yourself praise. Flex or check out your ass in front of the mirror. Understand that you got something done because you did it, not some amorphous collective helped you do it. Embrace your individuality; there is plenty of success in this world to take, the question is:

Are you going to be the one to take it?

I'll tell you who took it and used this so-called "malignant narcissism" to be one of the most successful men of all time: Donald Trump. Say what you like, but the man that used overwhelming optimism and positive thinking is now the one occupying 1600 Pennsylvania Ave. I would argue that the overwhelming vast majority of successful people in politics or business all have massive egos. Oh sure, you'll get the occasional person who hates themselves or self-flagellates and still wins, but I'd argue that the overwhelming vast majority that wins have pretty solid egos on them.

Vanity is awesome. Give yourself some credit. Flex in front of the mirror. When you have a success celebrate it.

Chapter XXI

The Spheres of Influence

One of the most influential concepts I ever came across that helped tighten up my mental game is the concept of Spheres of Influence that I saw at a work conference a long time ago. Usually, these conferences are a colossal sleepwalk through tedious meetings. One time though, I caught a real gem that really revolutionized the way I thought. Basically, the gist is this: Separate the things that happen in your life into three categories:

Category One: Things you directly control.
1. What pants I wear today.
2. What I eat today.
3. How much effort I put into my job.

Category Two: Things you don't control, but can influence.
1. Your Boss's perception of you.
2. Whether or not you got a date.
3. Traffic and whether or not I'm late to work.

Category Three: Things you do not control.
1. The Weather.
2. Accidents that happen to you.
3. A store being sold out of something.

So here's the deal. Learning to separate events into these categories really helped me get my mind in line. I used to worry so much about things weren't directly under my control. Learning how to do this one thing really adjusted my attitude:

Let it go.

No, I don't mean that insanely popular Frozen song, I mean learning how to respond to things that really you didn't influence in the first place. I've talked about learning to reframe, which is an excellent method to keep your attitude in check and stay positive. This is another one. I used to get so mad at things I didn't really control. Someone above me would make a decision that I hated, and I'd get so angry it would distract me for a long time. One of my favorite sayings is this:

It is what is.

If something happens to me that is entirely outside my control, I say it is what is, and deal with it. Now, here's the trick, recognizing whether or not something was TOTALLY out of your control, or whether or not you could have influenced it. Here's an example: Let's say you were late to work because you got caught in traffic. That's an obvious category three right? Wrong. You could have influenced that. You could have checked for an alternate route, GPS, checked the website to see if there was a scheduled bridge opening, left early, etc. There's a lot of things you could have done to influence whether or not you were late. So keep in mind, spare the "is what it is" stuff until you know for sure.

Here's a highly personal example I hate even to share. I once thought for sure I had herpes. I kissed a girl on a date once and found out after the fact she had herpes. I was devastated. I thought "My life is over" briefly, then I thought to myself "Well fuck it, it is what it is." Sure I could have influenced whether or not I got it, but that ship had already sailed. I moved almost immediately into acceptance. I started looking for HSV+ dating sites and medications. It turns out I didn't actually have it as I found out later, but I was pretty proud of the way I responded. A lot of people would have really sunk into despair, but I recognized the reality, and accepted it and moved on. The spheres of influence are very useful in instantly categorizing things and quickly addressing them. In this example, my reality was that I was going to have to live the rest of my life with Herpes. No amount of whining or crying was going to change it. There is no point whatsoever in crying over things you can't change. Learn to accept and then move on. From then on I always asked potential dates if they had any medical concerns I should be aware of, and actually caught it before it became a problem.

Another example is this: policies your boss hands down that you hate. Most people are passive and will take this sort of thing as a category 3 when in reality it's more like a category 2. Most people drastically underestimate how much influence they can have on their boss. You aren't just a lemming; you have to exert your influence at all times. If you boss implements a policy you hate, you have to think back to how many opportunities you had to make a difference. How many times did you not speak up when you saw something off? Or at the very least, what could you have done differently to change the outcome? It wasn't necessarily inevitable. The point is, learn to categorize and separate the things you can control, influence, or neither. Once you learn to do that, certain things will be much easier to accept. You can't control certain things, but you can control your reaction to them. Let's say you find out your significant other has been cheating on you. Well, clearly that's all their fault, isn't it? Not necessarily. There are a million actions you could have taken over time to lessen that probability. Learn to recognize what is a legitimate category 3 item, and the possibilities will open up in your mind about what you really could have influenced versus not. We will delve more into dating and relationships in a bit but for now, its time to learn how to Play to Win.

Chapter XXII

Playing to Win

I used to be a scrub.

I played a competitive card game called Magic the Gathering. I had designs to play professionally, as I loved the game, and still do to this day. It's an amazingly well-designed game with just the right amount of simplicity and mechanics. Anyway, I played A LOT. Virtually every waking moment I wasn't working I was immersed in this game. I played and tested over and over, with every conceivable variant of a card in my deck of 60 cards. I was a decent player, and I felt like I was above average at the game. I peaked out at top 10 in the state of Virginia, and very nearly qualified for the Pro Tour.

I had one critical flaw that I didn't realize till later, that likely cost me everything.

I was a scrub, and I wasn't playing to win.

Several years after my Magic career was over, I stumbled across a man named David Sirlin. He would become one of the most influential people in my life, and in my development of the concept of the Iron Mind. David is a World Champion player at the video game Street Fighter. He's a game designer, writer, among other things. David wrote an article, and a book that changed my life called Play to Win. In it, he detailed the concept of a scrub, which fit me to a tee. Essentially, a scrub is someone that has mentally handicapped themselves, and thus never becomes exceptional. The scrub invents reasons for losing, establishes a fictional set of guidelines that the game doesn't recognize, and generally doesn't do what's necessary to win.

Let me explain further. In Magic the Gathering, you build a deck of 60 cards mixed from a pool of hundreds, in some cases thousands of cards with goal of reducing your opponent's life from 20 to 0. Generally, the pros determine through massive amounts of testing what the best decks are, and those decks become the "metagame." People usually pick one of those decks to play and go to tournaments. There's also a class of player who likes to make their own decks, which refuse to use pro decks, who see it as beneath them to use one. I was in this class. I wanted to make my own deck, on my terms, and win the way I wanted to win. Unfortunately, the best decks are the best for a reason, and I never did well using my own stuff. However, I told myself what a fantastic person I was, because I was so much better than those people who just copied the pro decks. I invented excuse after excuse for losing, none of which were ever my fault of course.

Let me thoroughly detail for you here, my scrub behaviors:
1. Invented rules the game didn't recognize.
2. Refused to use the best cards/decks.
3. Blamed luck for my losses.
4. Refused to look at my own poor play.

I'm sure there's more. Let me explain a few of these. Inventing arbitrary rules is one of the worst offenses I've seen people make virtually every day. If you compete for something, whether it be a video game, contest at work, or a sporting event and you invent mental rules that don't exist within the game; you are a scrub. Let me elaborate. I'm going to use football since it's one of the more well-known sports. Let's say hypothetically you are a coach and you have a game coming up. You know from the scouting report that the opposing team is on their third-string cornerback, and you have one of the leagues top receivers. If you were to decide not to attack that corner because it wouldn't be fair, and you don't want to take advantage, congratulations, you're a scrub. Now, you never, ever see this, because scrub behavior rarely happens at the extreme highest level the NFL represents, so if you want to execute at the highest level, you have to be willing to operate at the highest tier.

Here's another that I experienced in real life. In my previous life, I worked in sales. We had a large number of metrics we were responsible for, including extended warranty sales. These warranties covered accidental damage, so if you shattered your phone screen, for example, it would be replaced. We had a group of people on our team that felt that exploiting the fear of breakage and using it to sell the warranty was underhanded and that we shouldn't do that, but to sell the value of the plan based on the high level of support they would receive.

That is pure scrub behavior.

Any cognitive scientist on the planet will tell you that fear is the highest grade persuasion tool in existence. If you intentionally leave out the best persuasion mechanism there is, you are artificially handicapping yourself. To sit there and suggest that you are just a better person because you didn't engage in this behavior that you consider to be beneath you is absurd. What you really did was invent an arbitrary rule that you used to cover for your mediocre results. "I may have failed, but look what a good person I am!" is the battle cry of the scrub. Also, you were willing to leave out relevant information on something that actually happens pretty regularly, I.E., a shattered phone screen. So you virtue signaled to make yourself feel better and ended up screwing both you and the customer. Then, on top of all that, using fear as a persuasion mechanism is in no way illegal. There is nothing wrong with it. All you did was artificially handicap yourself with something you wouldn't even get fired over.

I can't tell you how many people I've run across in my career that were supremely talented, but utterly lacked the will to win because they invented some rule whose only purpose was to make them feel better about themselves. Let's take a look at another scrub behavior: Blaming Luck. Magic, as I mentioned, is a card game. That means that is always going to be some element of randomness. Some games you are going draw all the right cards, and some games not at all, much like poker. I used to blame luck all the time. "Oh, I didn't draw enough of this that or the other thing" when in reality there were probably clearly a handful of plays I missed that could have turned things around. The other element to it, that I recognized in passing, but never thought about too much until later: The same people seemed to win consistently. For such a luck based game, the same people were winning pro tours over and over again. I've talked about cognitive dissonance, and this was a trigger for me. I'd complain about some luck-based event in the game, then immediately put out of my mind that the same people win consistently regardless. In any card game, there is going to be an element of luck, but the top performers are able to eliminate the mental blocks that prevent them from coming out ahead.

How many times have you watched a competitive sport or event, and watched someone or a team get lucky over and over? Probably a lot. There's always the teams that always seem to get the right bounce or the benefit of the doubt. There are invariably those people for whom things seem to play out the right way. Now, let's be realistic, there's a lot of luck in life. However, there's also a lot of creating your own luck. There's a lot of putting yourself in position to get lucky. Doing the work necessary to be in the right place for good things to happen. I'll go back to Magic, because it yields so many examples.

You made a deck of 60 cards, pulled from a pool of hundreds.

You have played with it a fair amount, and have won several local tournaments.

You decide to take it with you to a Regional or Pro event.

You do reasonably well, go 5-1 and you need a win to make it to the finals.

In the last match, you have each won one game, so the next game ends it.

You get your opponent down to 3 life.

You have a card in your deck that deals 3 damage, all you have to do is draw it.

You don't, and he kills you the next turn.

You lost the tournament, and win nothing.

Is this scenario rotten luck?

First, let's take a look at this scenario. On the surface, you just lost that game because you didn't draw a particular card. I've made this excuse a thousand times playing any number of games. "Well X didn't happen, and I got screwed. He got lucky, what can I do?" Ok, so let's take a look at the above scenario, and I will attempt to show the massive amount of ways out.

Out of the pool of hundreds of cards, are you sure you chose correctly?

How many decisions did you mess up in the three games total that led to that situation?

Did you correctly playtest enough and calculate the probabilities of drawing that card?

Did you play 3 of them instead of 4, decreasing odds of drawing it?

What happened in the game you lost earlier? You may not have needed to play this game at all.

Did you make any strange card choices when building the deck?

Did you bluff properly and establish good body language and visual cues?

There are a zillion variables that all lead to that moment. Another example is in football when someone gets mad at a kicker for missing the last kick to win the game. Did you play flawlessly up till that point? How many things occurred that should have taken you out of that situation entirely? So much of getting "lucky" is doing the hard work and laying the foundation to put the elements in play to get lucky.

The other part is setting aside what you think is "cheap" or in bad taste. One of my favorite stories Sirlin tells is how he won a Street Fighter tournament by using one character's move that he figured out beat all others. A lot of people would think to themselves, "hey that's kind of cheap to use the same move over and over like that." Thoughts like that are why he's a world champion, and you aren't. The reality is, the will to win at any cost is part of the equation too. Remember, there's no rule in the game that says you can't use the same move over and over. That's an arbitrary rule you made up in your head. If the optimal way to win is to use the same move over and over, then anything else is suboptimal, which makes it dumb to do if you are competing at that level.

I'm glad I watched the 2018 Super Bowl before publishing this book because that game was an absolute clinic by Doug Peterson on playing to win. He made gutsy call after gutsy call because he understood what he was up against, the Patriot machine. He showed up to win the game, not play not to lose.

I can't recommend enough that everyone read his book. If you do anything even remotely competitively, it's a must-read. However, it isn't enough to just play to win; we have to cultivate a winning mentality.

"I no longer grow agitated when I'm cornered. Nothing can mentally break me anymore. I have mastered nervousness and tension. I can instantly tell opponents apart and categorize them into groups and types according to their personality and weaknesses."

-Daigo "The Beast" Umehara, Street Fighter World Champion.

Chapter XXIII

Winning Mentality

"Winning is a habit, unfortunately so is losing."

-Vince Lombardi

A lot of people have no idea how accurate that quote is. Having a winning mind frame isn't just valuable to making you more confident in your ability, it's important also because it actively decreases the confidence of a significant amount of your opposition. Winning becomes something of a perpetual engine, that feeds into itself, and inhabits all those you face, filling you with confidence, and them with dread.

Arnold Schwarzenegger is one of the greatest ever to understand this principle. During his bodybuilding career, he learned to actively convince people that they were ready to lose to him. Watch Pumping Iron. This movie is a masterclass in the Iron Mind. He learned how to actively crush people, just by the perception that he was a winner. He understood that if your opponent THINKS you are a winner, then that can actively depress his confidence and change how he acts. Watch that movie, and watch Arnold literally talk people into being losers. It's astonishing to watch how supreme confidence and being a winner influences the people in his orbit. He said:

"If I find someone at a contest that's as good as me, or maybe even a bit better, I'll just spend some time with them. By the time I'm done, they will be ready to lose. I will talk them into it."

 Keep in mind as well:

There is no cheating in anything he's doing, or I'm advocating.

The beauty of all of this is that you are still playing within the rules or work, life, or the game. Using every tactic available to you within the rules, including psychological warfare on others, doesn't make you unethical, it makes you a winner. Do not allow someone else not having the Iron Mind weaken yours. When you arrive at the upper echelon of anything, the difference between number one and number two is infinitesimal. Undermining your opponent's mental state might only give you a one percent advantage, but sometimes one percent is enough to tip the scales, especially at the higher tiers of work or competition. Remember Active Assertive from the Iron Attitude chapter? An active assertive personality is going to be confident and very self assured. To them, winning is a habit, a foregone conclusion. That attitude not only powers their mind up, but actively suppresses others around them. If you want to succeed at the highest levels, these are the tools necessary.

I've been here before myself. In my career playing Magic the Gathering, I went to many tournaments, and I always did pretty well. Unfortunately back then I didn't have the same mind frame I do now, so I was never successful at the highest echelons of the game. I was, however, still an excellent tier 2 player. I went to a tournament once with a best friend at the time with whom I playtested the game endlessly. We knew each other's deck of cards inside and out. In a pool of hundreds of people, we were paired to play in the first round of the tournament. I could see his heart sink immediately as we walked up to the table and he came to the sinking realization that he had to play me. It was in that moment that knew I had him. He was mentally defeated before the game even started. My aura of being a higher tier player than him took him out before we even started. The game might as well have not even been played, as we both knew what was going to happen. Throughout the game, he made indecisive moves, poor decisions, and gave away things with body language. This was a prime example of someone being ready to lose, and I was merciless. It's not enough to recognize advantages that you have; you have to be willing to take advantage of them and actually win.

Another of my favorite quotes that's been said by everyone from Charles Barkley, to Larry Bird, to Brock Lesnar is:

"I hate to lose more than I like to win."

Therein lies the essence of a winning mentality. The utter refusal to accept anything mediocre. Someone with that attitude won't win every time, but you can bet your house they will win more than they lose. Once you start winning and building that aura, it permeates your being and everyone around you, becoming a self-fulfilling prophecy. However, despite all of this, there is an even bigger principle you must understand:

There is a difference between wanting to be a winner; and deciding to be a winner.

We all want a lot of things in life. We want a nice car or house, we want a great spouse, and we generally want to be a success in various pursuits. However, the difference between wanting and deciding to have something is astronomical. Once you've decided to do or have something, the end result is a foregone conclusion. The only variable is how much effort it's going to take to get it. Wanting something is wishy washy, it's just a desire that you aren't willing to manifest into the real world. Once you have decided to have something, then there's no stopping you because you've already determined what the end state will be, and no amount of pain or work is going to stop it. My Dad used to say something that I was reminded of by Scott Adams during a video stream, and was echoed by Ace Rothstein in the movie Casino:

> "No matter how big a guy might be, Nicky would take him on. You beat Nicky with fists, he comes back with a bat. You beat him with a knife, he comes back with a gun. And if you beat him with a gun, you better kill him, because he'll keep comin' back and back until one of you is dead.
>
> -Ace Rothstein, Casino

In the quote above, Ace outlines what happens when Nicky "decides" to fight someone. Nicky doesn't WANT to win, he DECIDES he's going to win. If that means he has to take multiple trips to the hospital or even the morgue, the cost doesn't matter, because the decision is made. Now, how do we apply this to non-fighting scenarios? You have to decide to win at life, in whatever challenge you decide to take on. Don't want to do something and then half-ass your way through it; decide to have it, and pay the price to get it. People like Jordan, Kobe, Trump, they all decided to become great, and embraced the grind of work to make it happen. Here's another example: the very book you are reading right now. I had never written anything even remotely resembling a book or even a blog. I had no reason to believe I was even capable of writing a book, but I DECIDED to write one. Once the decision was made, it was going to happen; now, hundreds of hours later, it is in your hands. I never stopped to think "Man, I want to write a book, but I have no experience doing this, it's probably too much work." Once the decision was made, the end result was set in stone.

You can decide to be a winner. Never think otherwise.

Now we understand what being a winner and playing to win is all about, so let's see how we should ethically handle this newfound mentality.

Chapter XXIV

Learn to Play the Game

"Never attempt to win by force what can be won by deception."

-Niccolò Machiavelli, The Prince

After all this talk of hardcore winning mentality, assertiveness, and playing to win, you might be thinking to yourself, "How far should I take this?" Now, if you've read The Prince by Machiavelli or 48 Laws of Power, you know that things can get really dicey ethically. You'll be presented with opportunities to take advantage of people, situations, and be in a position to do some filthy things. If you've ever heard the term "Machiavellian," then you have an idea what I'm talking about. Machiavelli was famous for lauding tactics with some shall we say….questionable ethics. Now, remember, a large part of the Iron Mind is keeping stress and controllable tension to a minimum. Thus I advocate the following rule:

Do anything to win within the rules.

It's really that simple. Let me break this down further. Generally speaking, I'm a really ethical guy. If you asked me what the worst thing I've ever done is, I don't have a quick answer. I'd probably have to go back to high school when I was a kid to find something serious like stealing a pack of gum. The point is, rigid adherence to the rules as it relates to ethical decisions will keep you clean and out of trouble.

Where I switch it up is in the area of what I call adherence decisions. Adherence decisions are those decisions that are mostly annoying process decisions, anything that falls outside the realm of ethics. Those are the decisions you can really find some room to work with. Think of it like this:

If you are 100% sure you won't get fired for it, no one gets hurt, and you think it's a good move, then do it.

Here's the thing. Most people are yes men. Most people tell others (boss or significant other) what they think they want to hear and don't take any leeway outside the simple rules. What I'm saying is that sometimes justifiably breaking a rule that won't get you fired or divorced makes you look terrific to your boss or significant other. It makes you look like a winner to flout a rule here and there and come out ahead for having done it. Now, you have to have a good reason, and be prepared to fight for it. I talked in the Iron attitude chapter about never apologizing, and here's where it comes in. If you have an idea or something that is demonstrably better than what's being done, and you have to break a rule to do it, go for it. Especially if you know you won't get fired over it. Taking the initiative in this way makes you look like an innovator, like someone who gets things done.

Now let's have some real talk: You are going to be surrounded by people looking to screw you, especially in the workplace. One of the biggest mistakes you can make, and that I've made myself is not recognizing when someone is running game on you. I've had it happen many times. In my younger years, I assumed the best of everyone. I was always a pretty ethical guy, so I thought everyone else had the sort of innate

goodness I had. I had to learn the hard way that there are a lot of real scumbags out there. In some cases, I have been betrayed by friends that I've had for years. Do not let your perception be clouded. Learn to recognize when things aren't adding up with one of your friends or even family. Recognize the signs that they are working against your interests and if necessary confront them. Learn to recognize body language and speech patterns. For example, learn to spot dishonest denials. If you ask me if I murdered someone I might have two answers:
1. No, of course not, that's absurd.
2. Why, who told you that? Where did you hear such a thing?

One of those is a lot more credible denial than the other, and it should be obvious it's the first. Learn to spot things like this. Do not allow someone to take advantage of you, or play political games on you at work or in your personal life. There are always going to be people trying to get over on you. Forever be mindful of the games. This is why I absolutely advocate reading The Prince and 48 Laws of Power. If for no other reason, even if you plan on staying 100% ethical, they will allow you to recognize when people are doing shady things to you. I've seen a lot of outstanding people get absolutely taken advantage of because they didn't understand inter-office politics and deceptive maneuvers. I'm going to tell you something that is going to sound really nihilistic:

Give no one the benefit of the doubt.

Trust is a precious commodity, and it has to be earned. It can't be bought or stolen. Do not under any circumstances give anyone the benefit of the doubt unless they have won it. Even then, you have to watch out for your own interests first. There is nothing selfish about making sure you aren't getting screwed. I've had pretty close friends that absolutely tried to take advantage of me, and I'm quite sure you have as well. Learning to recognize when someone is running game on you is absolutely a learned skill.

Do not say more than necessary.

I cannot tell you how many times I've seen people hang themselves with their own words. I've seen people do something totally justifiable and absolutely better than what was being done, completely blow it by talking too much. Here's the problem with over communicating: You are providing ammunition for the other person. By keeping your explanations concise and focused, you present what information is necessary without bringing in another element that could be harmful to your position. For example, I worked with a girl once; I will call her Sally. Sally was extremely affable and pleasant to be around, and everyone liked her. Except for one: the Boss. Sally, for all her amazing interpersonal skills, wasn't really great at the job. Then on top of that, the boss didn't really like her either. She would call me once in awhile in tears after getting harsh criticism from the boss about something or another, and after listening to her talk for a good 15 minutes, I started to isolate the problem:

She was providing negative information about herself to the boss, that was well beyond the scope of the original topic. Here's how the process would go, he would call her out for something minor, and she'd spend 20 minutes trying to explain it, and in the process uncover another six things she did wrong or even something in her personal life that was a problem, thus lowering the bosses confidence in her. In other words, she was handing him the rope with which he was hanging her constantly. The moral of the story is this: Be ready with a quick, defensible, concise, and focused response in scenarios like this, do not crucify yourself with your own words.

Learn everyone's weakness.

Everyone has a way they can be bent to your will without resorting to lying or deceit. As we learned in the chapter on Lenses, every single person walking this earth has a world view and a line of lenses. Figuring out what they are for each person is the trick. You have to learn how to approach each person you interact with in a manner that is going to get results. Approaching me with an idea is a very different operation than approaching say, my mom. It is beyond critical, and I say this having made this mistake hundreds of times over, to tailor your approach to the person you are dealing with. Learn about people, their likes, dislikes, pet peeves, hot buttons, and attitude, and you will have a key to get whatever you want. Some might look at this as manipulation, I look at it as effective and smart. If you can do this properly, you will immediately be ahead of 90% of the people you know. Here's an example:

Lets say you have a proposal for an expansion of your product line, but you need the supervisor's approval to go forward. The first thing you need to do is determine what motivates your boss, and what kind of person he/she is. This is where most fail, they just look at the presentation first, and don't tailor it specifically to the audience. We talked about this in the Frame games chapter. If you have a Type A personality or brash and ambitious boss, you do not want to go into that presentation with a bunch of bland numbers and statistics. You will bore them to death and they will start playing games on their phone while you talk (yes, I've seen this firsthand). A Type A boss wants to know that what you are proposing is going to help them WIN. Learn about them. Maybe they need a big promotion to pay for that second mortgage, or on a boat they overspent. Focus on the feeling of winning, not bland statistics. Paint the picture of how your idea is going to help them win more at life, not how awesome you are at Excel. Conversely, if your boss is a numbers oriented person, go in there with dazzling charts and show massive percentages and how awesome you are going to make the numbers.

I say again: This is not manipulation. This is just smart. Do not invent a set of rules for yourself to play by that don't exist. We already talked about scrubs. Do not be one. Learning how to present to individual's personalities, not as though they are all the same, will change the game for you. Go back and reread that chapter on the Lenses of Life, if you can figure out other people's lenses, you will have a significant edge in any dealings.

Learn about people, and they will provide you the tools you need to tell them what they want to hear.

Chapter XXV

The Pence Process

It's March 30, 2017. Mike Pence, Vice President of the United States, makes a comment off the cuff about how he doesn't dine alone with women who aren't his wife. Cue the internet and feminist firestorm:

"How Mike Pence is Hurting Women"

"We are all shocked."

"Just don't sexually harass women."

"Women's progress suffers."

And on and on. Article after article savaging Pence left and right for the heretical notion he has about respecting his wife. As I write this, it's now November 30, 2017, and we are in the middle of a sexual harassment firestorm among the media, Hollywood, and Congress. Al Franken, Harvey Weinstein, Matt Lauer, John Conyers, Kevin Spacey are just a tiny fraction of those caught in harassment claims over a month or two. Every day that passes, there's another one going down, and Mike Pence looks more and more like a genius everyday because I can tell you who ISN'T getting a harassment claim:

Mike Pence.

There's more to it though, and I've given it a name, the Pence Process. Some call it the Pence Rule, but that only applies to interactions with his wife. I want to broaden it out quite a bit.

The Pence Process is any process that we undertake that removes our willpower and temptation from the equation of what we are trying to do. Let me explain. Mike Pence might be doing this just to respect his wife, or because of his religion, but he's also gaining other benefits from this policy of his.

1. He has a ZERO percent chance of temptation.
2. Willpower is removed from the equation.
3. False accusations are borderline impossible.
4. Solidifies the relationship with his wife.
5. Makes her feel extremely special.
6. It doesn't even cross her mind he might cheat.

Look at all those benefits he accrues from that one policy. On the surface, it sounds disrespectful of women, like something someone in the 1950s would do. However, I can't stress enough how important it is that he has removed willpower from the equation. I'm going to teach you how to use the Pence Process in other areas of your life. Listen, the reality is, a lot of the things I'm talking about are very, very difficult. Willpower on anything we WANT to do is a tough thing. I want to eat like shit all day. I want to have a lot of sex. Refraining from stuff you want to do is way harder than abstaining from things you don't actually like.

So how can we devise our own "Pence Process" for other things in our life? How can we implement processes that remove willpower (as much as possible) from the equation? Well, let's isolate that we need willpower for primarily. The first is relationships, and Mike has graciously shown us how to make your wife feel ultra special and eliminate temptation.

What else? How about one of the absolute most difficult tests of all:

Diet.

Working out is much less demanding than diet. You might work out for an hour in a day, but that leaves about 15 other waking hours in the day you need to be disciplined. Later on in the diet chapter, I'll nail down actual foods and programs and whatnot, but for now, how can we implement a Pence Process for dieting? Removing willpower from 15 hours of daily dieting is tough, but what if you could reduce it down to about 30 minutes, once a week? Remember the point of the Pence Process is to remove temptation, in other words, don't have it around. I'm talking of course about the food in your house. If it isn't there, your willpower has a much stronger likelihood of surviving. All you have to do is be disciplined for 30 minutes a week, in one location:

The grocery store.

That's right. I have major problems being disciplined on my diet while I sit around the house. I can, however, be super controlled in the grocery store, which largely eliminated the need for me to be restrained at home. What about working out though? How can we possibly reduce willpower necessary for that? Well here's another tip: Do cardio throughout the day instead of running on the treadmill consistently. Try to get in 15000 steps a day or so, and you won't need to bust ass as hard doing cardio in the gym. Personally, I hate cardio on a machine. I'd rather walk in the woods with the dog, or even down the street. As part of the Pence Process, you can also substitute something you hate, for more of something you don't entirely hate.

Here's another Pence Process I use: I don't drink. At all. Ever. This has similarity to what Pence does with wife in that they are both absolutes. If you leave wiggle room, you'll find ways to justify or loophole your way out of something. I prefer to deal in absolutes, especially with vices. I give myself no wiggle room on my policy at all, and neither does Mike Pence. Thus we reduce the chance of screwing up. Set the system in your head as a no-compromise absolute, and you make it much easier to follow. This reminds me of Catholic Dogma. You would think that the more ritualistic the religious practice is, the less likely people would be to follow it because it's hard. It's actually the opposite. People like some degree of order and ritual, so the church found that the harder the dogma was, the more it retained believers. As the church relaxed its dogma over the years, people became less devout and more likely to stray.

Here's another example. When I first ventured out on my own to start my business, I decided I was going to do a Periscope Live Stream every single day. I did exactly that. For six months I don't think I missed a single day. I set it as an absolute, something that I wasn't going to deviate from no matter what. At some point, I decided to give myself one day off. Once I broke the streak, it was as if I had permitted myself not to do them every day. All of a sudden, I would make an excuse to miss one here and there. Missing one day a week spiraled into a few days a week, and my viewership went down. Once you permit yourself to break the process, it can result in further degradations of your goals. Now, that is a separate question from whether I should have been doing Periscopes every day in the first place, but I can tell you making something an absolute definitely works to strengthen your resolve and stay on track.

Deal in absolutes. Some will advise otherwise, I'm telling you it works. In the next chapter, we are going to create our own dogma and rituals.

Chapter XXVI

Become the Machine

"We are what we repeatedly do. Excellence, then, is not an act, but a habit."

-Aristotle

Have you ever noticed that people in very dogmatic religions seem to have more willpower than others? Think about it. Take the Sikhs, with their incredibly ritualistic processes, fancy attire, perfect turbans, and beards. Or, how many obese Muslims have you ever seen? Same with hardcore Catholics and Christians. Now I'm not talking about the fly by night bandwagon people; I'm talking the most hardcore of each religion. Generally speaking, they have the Iron Mind. Why? Because they learned to submit to the dogma of their faith, and their mind has locked in on what the religion tells them to do. For them, a deviation isn't just undesirable; it's not even an option. You may or may not be religious; I don't care. What I do care about is using religious-style dogma to ramp you up to another level. Let's take a look at developing rituals.

I've always been very ritualistic. I like to get into a routine, and not deviate. You must learn to do this as well. Establishing rituals in your daily life will help to solidify the healthy habits and eliminate the bad ones. Everyone has routines that they perform daily; what you need to do is knowingly establish new ones. I never really thought about it much when I was growing up. I would do things in the same order every day, but I didn't recognize the habits I was building. I can't stress enough how significant it is to create good practices and rituals. Keep this in mind as well:

> *"Life is a series of habits, Changing one little habit is often the difference between a great life and a mediocre existence. One habit can be the tiny support for many other destructive behaviors."*
>
> -Ed Latimore

In the Toxicity Audit chapter, we learned we have to get rid of old bad habits, so now let's take a look at building good habits.

Here are some examples of my morning ritual:
1. Wake up at the same time every day, unless extenuating circumstances prevent.
2. Take a few deep breaths.
3. Immediately roll out of bed and turn the fan off (I can barely sleep without a fan.)
4. Go to the bathroom and tie my hair back.
5. Take a couple of anti-inflammatories.
6. Put my watch on and get my phone from the bedside.
7. Turn off light and walk down the hallway to turn the thermostat back up to 76, from 69, my sleeping temperature.
8. Grab the dog's bowl and give him food, and make sure he has water.

9. Prepare my caffeinated pre-activity drink (This can be coffee for you, but I hate coffee.)
10. Sit in my chair and scan Twitter for news that occurred while I slept.
11. Go back to the bedroom and get dressed.
12. Walk the dog.
13. While walking, breathe and take in everything and analyze the day.
14. If it's a non-workout day, return and make breakfast and morning drink.
15. If it's a workout day, use foam roller and stretch.
16. Proceed to next ritual.

This is a ritual that occurs pretty much every day. We all have rituals in our life, whether it be how we shower, or how we mow the lawn. We generally don't put much thought into these things; we just do them unconsciously. What I'm telling you to do is knowingly create rituals. Create them for everything, and learn to tailor them to get positive results. We pick up habits and rituals all the time; we just don't recognize that we do. It's critical to get on the right path with your mind, to establish rituals in your everyday life. Reward yourself for fulfilling them a certain amount of times if you have to.

I'm a big believer in reward systems. It's a proven fact that rewards are sweeter the harder they are to get, so they can't be easy to achieve. That's the mistake a lot of people make, is that they use rewards for every insignificant achievement. "Oh I worked out today, so now I get to eat a Big Mac." No. These are all conscious decisions that you have to make. The more set in stone the reward system is, the more likely you are to stick to it. The Iron Mind knows that a specific ritual set will benefit, so it locks into these rituals and makes them immutable.

When I was younger, I was driven by rage. I was mad at everything and everyone. I was irate at not having better genetics. I was angry at women for not seeing how obviously great of a guy I was. One way my rage did benefit me though, was in my workout. I was a machine at going to the gym. I was working out six days a week, on the same timetable and ritual every day, and beating myself up for not going on the seventh day. Looking back, I did a lot of things wrong, but the one thing I did right was to have immutable rituals. Just as you saw my morning ritual above, it was mainly the same except the gym was on it virtually every day. I was also very good at dieting. My rituals absolutely applied to food, and I had no problem eating the same things over and over and getting into a routine. We will talk more about diet later.

Now I'm sure some are saying "Hey I'm not this type of person, I'm spontaneous and free-spirited, I can't lock myself into rituals like that." That's where you are wrong. That thought pattern is inherently self-limiting, and keeping you from being the best version of yourself. Myself, I'm a massive introvert. I can quite literally be alone for weeks at a time and have no problem with it. I used to tell myself, "Well, this is just the way you are, you can't help it." Again, extremely self-limiting. Over the years, I've gotten much better at socializing and very good at public speaking. You have to understand that what you think, is what you will make true. There's a lot of self-fulfilling prophecy in life. If you believe a certain thing about yourself, you are very likely to find ways to make it true. We see this all the time, in action. How often do you hear people say something to the effect of "Well I can't do that anymore, I'm getting old." Now, that bears some truth. Once you get to a super advanced age, you can't do certain things. The problem is, I hear that from 40-year-olds occasionally, and yet I've met 60-year-olds who climb mountains. Every gym has that 70-year-old guy that's super ripped. If you believe something like that about yourself, you will make it come true. There is more self-fulfilling prophecy than most people understand in life.

Part of believing in yourself more strongly, are rituals. Following rituals will give you that sense of achievement and allow you to understand that you can do, and be more. Have a set ritual, but leave a few steps open for change. Let's take a look at a gym ritual:

1. Arrive at the Gym
2. Go to the bathroom to ensure no interruptions.
3. Put on headphones.
4. Cue up warmup playlist of escalating intensity.
5. 5 minute Stretch routine
6. 10 Minute Cardio to warm up.
7. Workout program (weights or Yoga)
8. 20 Minute Cardio to finish.

So in there we definitely have a ritual. What we also have is the ability to change what type of workout, and what kind of cardio we do. This will fluctuate depending on what you try to achieve of course, but the principle stays the same. Another thing I recommend is keeping others out of your rituals as much as you can. The gym is a prime example. I'm a big believer in working out by yourself. I prefer to be in a workout zone, and I will talk more about that later. If you involve another person in your ritual, especially your gym ritual, you had better be completely sure they are as dedicated, if not more so, than you are. Do not let another person break your ritual. I know people who rely heavily on another, and if that person doesn't come through, it really devastates them. This is your Iron Mind we are building, not someone else's.

Now here's another thing about rituals. Once you achieve what you want, you can roll back some of the more hardcore ones. I am nowhere near as ritualistic as I used to be. Back in my earlier days, I used to prepare a week's worth of meals, and eat the same thing every day. Holidays didn't even really matter much to me back then. I was at the gym no matter if I was sick, or even in the most inclement weather. I was unbreakable because that's what I needed to be at the time. Life is all phases. When I was young and told something I was doing was a phase, I used to get incensed. How dare these people tell me what I'm supposed to be doing. Everything in life is a phase, to some degree. You might be in the same phase for 50 years, but it's still a phase. Everyone evolves to some degree, I can tell you I have some of the same core principles I had at 20, but I've gone through a lot of changes. Nowadays, I still eat clean most of the time, but I'm not nearly as hardcore as I once was.

I would not recommend going as hard as I did back in the day, unless you are a performance athlete. I gave up everything: girls, holidays, and family to try to become an unbreakable machine. To a large degree I was, but I wouldn't recommend that for most people. You do however have to be hardcore enough to build habits. When I first started, going to the gym and dieting was pure misery, now I relish it. Once you build a habit that makes you feel good, and you've built the Iron Mind, things you used to hate will become great sources of pleasure for you. I've gotten to the point where I love working out, and will still be doing it until I'm dead. Remember most things are a cycle. If you work out, you feel better; and if you feel better, you'll work out more. Conversely, not working out makes you lazy and depressed, and yet you're lazy and depressed because you don't work out. Recognize cycles. I've gotten pretty good at catching myself if I feel a cycle is coming on. Remember, the ritual you devise has to be tough enough that you can ritualize it, if it's too easy it will become harder to stick to and internalize.

Remember, we already have rituals to some degree. The trick is to manipulate the ones you have into ones that are more beneficial for you. For example, if you go to work, you have to park your car. I'd recommend parking in the furthest possible spot and walk. Park in the same spot every day if possible. I do this everywhere I go. Think about how much you drive, now imagine how many steps you could add to your routine over a month if you parked further away. It's actually a lot; I'm very rarely below 20,000 steps a day. It's little things like this that will put you position to get where you want to go. They all add up; the little rituals will pile up day after day, month after month, all towards the goal of making a better version of you and your Iron Mind.

Another ritual I've established recently is one of breathing. I had what I thought was shortness of breath, as it seemed I got winded too fast and was always sucking air. It turns out I just wasn't breathing correctly. I was taking ragged, short breaths continually, and holding it too much. So, I endeavored to see if I could change that, and I did. Now, upon both waking and going to bed, I do five cycles of breathing. 4 seconds inhale through my nose, 7-seconds hold, and 8 second breathe out through the mouth. I've also become far more cognizant of breathing during working out, and it's helped immensely. I also do these exercises on my morning dog walk, and it's great to get that morning air worked into my lungs.

We will look more into breathing later, but for now, understand the broader point:

Rituals work.

Chapter XXVII

The War on Cigarettes

One of the hardest mental tests I've ever had was quitting smoking. Here's the thing, quitting something you really like is damn hard. Refraining from drinking and drugs is easy for me because I don't like either of them. It doesn't take willpower to quit or not do something you don't like, with the possible exception of dodging peer pressure. Smoking, I absolutely love. I'm not even kidding, it's one of my favorite things to do, ever. For me, smoking is a tremendous relaxer. It forces me to stop and reflect for a moment especially in stressful situations. It allowed me to calm down, chill out, then get back to what I was doing with renewed focus. The best shape I was ever in, I was smoking like an absolute chimney. I'd literally sit outside the gym, before and after a workout, and smoke cigarettes. I find quitting smoking much harder than dieting because even on a diet, you can still reward yourself with a pizza once in awhile, and it's not like you stop eating entirely.

As I got older, the health negatives became more apparent. Besides the lung issues, I also had reason to believe it was killing my circulation[1]. I loved smoking, but I knew what I'd have to do. For a lot of years, I talked myself out of quitting, because I worked in customer service, and without cigarettes, my temper would boil over, and I'd get into fights with customers. So, I realized I'd need to reframe the issue. In the section on tactics, I talked about reframing, and this was a perfect opportunity to test it. The way I reframed the smoking issue was to take it as a direct challenge to my willpower. Since I knew the amorphous health issues that might or might not occur 30 years down the road were insufficient to get me to quit over the years, I decided to attack it this way:

Is my will too weak to quit smoking?

I know guys that are 80 years old and still smoke like chimneys. I actually worked with a guy who was 65 and had smoked filter-less cigarettes his entire life. He should have been dead 50 times over by then. So the health issues that might not even happen at all weren't enough to motivate me to quit. Being what I considered a tough guy with incredible dedication to working out and dieting, I couldn't stomach the fact that my will was too weak to stop smoking. So, while avoiding the possibility of lung cancer didn't really phase me or motivate me to quit, this did. I always prided myself on having an unbreakable will, so the idea that something could break it was unacceptable to me. So I decided to set out to prove my will could beat smoking. This is an example of finding something that does motivate you and spinning it into the right frame to conquer whatever it is. So great was my desire to prove how resilient my willpower was, it actually made it true. I went cold turkey off cigarettes one day, and a routine dose of affirmations and breathing exercises kept me sane.

I had another trick up my sleeve. The mechanics. I realized part of the appeal of smoking was the mechanical action of raising something up to my mouth and hanging onto it with my lips. Driving down the road, sitting in my chair, it didn't matter. I was addicted to the mechanics in addition to the actual nicotine. So, I knew I'd need a substitute. Something that could mimic the mechanical action of raising and lowering a cigarette and something that I could hold in my lips like one. I found the perfect analogue:

A pretzel rod.

That's right; the best quitting smoking companion ever turned out to be a pretzel rod. Slightly thicker than a cigarette, and much tastier, this allowed me to mimic the action of smoking and really helped a lot. Remember, it's all about putting yourself in position to succeed, and taking into account every aspect to help you win. So it all added up to a very successful outing. Always look for every edge you can get to motivate yourself.

Challenge + Affirmations + Breathing + Pretzels = Winning combination.

Chapter XXVIII

Annihilating Stress

If we are going to forge the Iron Mind, we have to find a way to obliterate stress. In this chapter, I'm going to outline a few things that have worked for me, or in general to blast away tension. Now, if you've been following directions, then you are already on the path to a minimal stress existence due to to a lot of the techniques I've laid out earlier, such as the toxicity audit. However, let's be honest, there is going to be stress if you exist on this planet. Very few people, even those who are wealthy, can lead a stress-free existence. With that in mind, how can eliminate the most amount of stress possible in the shortest amount of time? What activities are optimized for crushing stress?

Let's start with one of the big hitters of stress removal:

Guns. Big guns, preferably.

Shooting is really difficult to beat in the stress removal department. Feeling the power emanating from a gun barrel as it bucks in your hand is hard to beat. It's almost like you are actually shooting the stress out of your body via the gun barrel. I'm fortunate enough to live in the woods, so I can just go out back whenever I feel like it and shoot a few rounds. Most of you don't have that luxury. Find a range. Get good with a gun, because there are a few more elements to owning a firearm that ensure a stress-free existence. One, you know what's really stressful? Getting mugged or raped. Having a gun just might prevent all manner of negative things such as these from happening to you. I have heard that getting murdered is a fairly stressful event.

Guess what though; there's another element to it. Just the act of owning a gun and having it in the vicinity is a stress reducer in and of itself. Just its presence cleans up a lot of ancillary stress in your life. I didn't realize this until I forgot to renew my concealed carry permit. I had to go the courthouse and renew and found out the hard way that it was going to take 30-45 days to get it back. As a result, I had to stop carrying it and remove it from my vehicle. It's hard to overstate the difference I felt not having it around. I found that my degree of worrying was a few percentage points higher without it. I wouldn't say I was worried all the time, but I was a lot more worried than I was when I knew it was around. So yeah, just the act of owning a gun decreases stress I'd say a noticeable amount. Then actually shooting it further reduces stress. So get a gun, I promise it will help.

Vigorous Exercise.

This is the most obvious paragraph I'm likely to write in this book. I hope it's obvious to even someone who doesn't work out, that working out and exerting effort is going to eliminate stress. As I've mentioned, vigorous exercise produces endorphins that make us feel good. Getting the music thundering, the endorphins and blood cranking will do wonders. More on this in an upcoming chapter.

Have Sex.

I hope this is self-explanatory, if it isn't you should probably stop being a virgin.

The Serenity of Nature.

Walking in nature can literally rewire your brain.[1] Personally, I can't possibly feel less stressed than when I am walking a forest path on a beautiful day. That is maximal serenity for me. Now, as I've said, everyone is different. What works for one might not work for all, but as the footnote above talks about, it is 100% possible to rewire and get neurons firing by walking in nature. For me, this one is hard to beat. Eliminating all the "city sounds" like cars and just absorbing the peaceful serenity of the woods purges the stress levels from me. I'm going to talk more about breathing later, but once you get in the woods and get your lungs full of that pure air that one finds in the woods, it truly is another level.

I grew up in a small suburb without a lot of nature or woods surrounding me. For most of my life, I lived either in or around the city. There was rarely a time that I didn't hear cars, aircraft, people, and all manner of "city sounds." As I got older, I got progressively more disenchanted with the city. I'd get neighbors blasting their music through my paper thin walls, sirens at all hours of the night, the constant sound of people coming and going. Eventually, I'd had enough, and bought a house out near the country with a lot of woods around me. It is impossible to overstate the difference this made in my life. I immediately had lower stress levels, higher happiness levels, and my ability to relax multiplied tenfold. One of the best decisions I ever made, and frankly, I wish I'd

---

[1] https://well.blogs.nytimes.com/2015/07/22/how-nature-changes-the-brain/?mtrref=www.bing.com&gwh=C98086C9E7169803CCB4419D98F7A1D0&gwt=pay

have done it a long time ago. I can walk in the woods every day, shoot guns out back, and hear virtually no "city sounds" at all, not even cars. And it's amazing. Also, I got all this and managed to be 10 minutes from a Wal-Mart, so it's not like I'm totally outside of civilization.

Connect with nature; it's worth it.

Write it out.

I have to say; I never thought I'd be the one sitting here writing a book. This very act would have been incomprehensible to me ten years ago. That all changed when I started using Day One to journal on my iPhone and iPad. After a laborious day, or even a good one, I would drop bombs on people in my journal. Did someone piss me off that day? I'd pulverize them with words in my journal. I started doing entries for movies, games, books, the whole deal. Getting things out on paper or through writing certainly can help purge stress and get things off your mind. Keep in mind; there is absolutely evidence that writing can make us more mindful, and help remove stress.[2] Even if it's a small sentence or two in a journal, try it out. I bet you anything it will help. If you need to call your boss a dickhead, or a movie total shit, just do it. Get those feelings out and watch how much it helps once you've stopped internalizing them. Feel free to exaggerate too. If someone slightly annoyed you, absolutely

---

[2] https://www.health.harvard.edu/healthbeat/writing-about-emotions-may-ease-stress-and-trauma

eviscerate them with words. If a meal was mediocre, make it sound like the biggest shit sandwich of all time.

Getting feelings out in a variety of ways really helps present stress levels, but it also allows Future You to remember and understand things better. Become an expert at disintegrating stress as quickly and efficiently as possible.

Chapter XXIX

The Overrated List

For this chapter, I'm going to put forward a list of skills, behaviors, concepts or traits that I believe are massively overrated. I'm talking about stuff that virtually everyone seems to think are consensus, which have real opposition in a lot of circles. So let's get started with my number one most overrated skill:

Multi-tasking.

This one has got to be one of my biggest pet peeves. Everyone assumes, as should be logical, that multiple things have to be better than one thing! It's obvious, isn't it? It's right there in the name, why would you want to focus on one thing, when you could totally concentrate on several? There was a time when multitasking used to be the holy grail at work. Everyone wanted to be good at multitasking in the corporate world. I was obsessed with it. I tried to pack my computer screen with as many icons and windows as I possibly could, to try to absorb every nugget of information as quickly as possible. My eyes darted all across the screen at the faintest flicker of a useful piece of information. I'd carry on entire conversations with people while checking and reading texts and emails on my phone, all in pursuit of the ultimate corporate world prize: being a great multitasker.

Then I met someone who singlehandedly changed my view on it. I'll call her Mary. Mary was the "best" multitasker I'd ever seen. She could handle multiple projects at a time, carry on an entire conversation on two phones at once, always reading emails and texts while carrying on a conversation, the works. She was so good at it that it made me realize it isn't that great of a skill. Why? Because everyone felt ignored by her. Everyone felt unimportant. She never gave anyone more than two seconds of focus, and thus it made everyone dislike her. I recall trying to get her to focus on issues I had, and it was near impossible. She was always on the phone, always reading a mail, and would miss crucial details. Also, while all this was going on, I started doing a bit of writing. In the process of doing some writing, I noticed a couple of applications had "distraction free" modes. Basically, modes that removed all the icons and just presented you with a blank page to write on. I was baffled by this. Why would anyone want a blank page?

Then I tried it, and my ability and focus exploded. Trying to focus on so many things at once was taking away my ability to focus and drill down to the essence of my thinking. I thought about how much it annoyed me to talk to Mary, and how no one liked her because they never felt like she gave them any attention. When everything is urgent, nothing is; as the saying goes. I became obsessed with productivity methods, and the more I focused in on one thing, the more Zen and productive I became. This is how the iPad became my favorite computing device of all time. The genius of the iPad is that once you enter an application, the interface disappears. The iPad **becomes** the application. Unlike other tablets that try to retain elements of the operating system on the screen, the iPad eliminated them all and becomes a canvas for creativity. I feel more attached to the content that I'm generating on the iPad, and that's a big reason why.

Eliminate distraction. TV on in the background? Kill it. Do notifications keep popping up? Do not disturb mode. Even music. Switch to instrumentals for compositions and creativity, this is a time not to focus on lyrics, but on your content. Clean up your process, and you will engage yourself and your mind at a much higher level. Single-tasking and prime focus are where you want to be. Being disorganized and lacking focus isn't a winning strategy. Recognize this: activity is not an accomplishment, and it isn't quality either.

As it turns out, there is significant science[1] that shows that not only is Multitasking worse than Monotasking, but actually rewires our brains to make us less creative, and less efficient managers, thus proving what I only had thought of organically.

Learn to separate your processes.

Work smart, not hard.

This has got to be one of my absolute least favorite trends that popped up in the 80's and 90's. This is another example of something that appears to be unmistakably better on the surface. Who doesn't want to work smart? Who wouldn't rather find a more comfortable way around a difficult problem? I mean, I don't know about you, but I hate working dumb and hard. Again though, just like multitasking, something that looks obviously better on the surface isn't necessarily. Initially, in concept, I had no problem with this

---

[1] http://www.businessinsider.com/monotasking-better-than-multitasking-2017-3?r=UK&IR=T

line. The idea was to be smart and figure out the best way to do things without breaking your back over it. The problem that developed eventually with this phrase is that it came to mean find ways not to work hard at all. In the late 80's we started to see this narrative form that hard work was beneath you. We started telling our kids that "Hey, you don't want to be like that guy." That guy being the plumber or the pipe fitter that busts their ass, but makes a good living and raises a great family. Not only that, those guys get paid. The tradesmen I know make serious money, a lot more than most of the people that denigrate them.

The implication started to become that if you didn't go to college, then *the horror*, you might have to actually do a job that required physical labor. It also started to denigrate the idea of working hard, which led us to the entitled generation we have now. Keep in mind, everyone at the highest level works hard. There's no such thing as being successful without it unless you are a lottery winner. Every single successful person you know has busted their butt in some way to get there. To suggest to people, especially kids, that anything is going to come as a result of not working hard is doing them, and everyone around them, a disservice. The rest of us don't want to deal with your entitled brats.

My dad taught me a lesson many years ago I've never forgotten. When I was about 12 years old, the neighbor, Dennis was overhauling his lawn. As a favor to my dad to get me something to do, Dennis told me he'd pay me 20 dollars an hour to come over and rip up roots. I said Ok and went over there the next morning. His entire lawn was a mass of roots. I picked and picked, and it just seemed like I wasn't even making a dent. After an hour or two, I called it a day. Hey, what can I say, I was lazy back then. The next day I did maybe an hour or two, tops. After that I just kind of let it fade away. So, all in all, I spent maybe 4 hours pulling up roots in this guy's yard. I got my 80 bucks or so and patted myself on the back and went about my business.

I was huge into video games back then and had just gotten the first ever Nintendo Gameboy for Christmas. It was still reasonably new, so there wasn't a vast library of games available. As I perused the latest issue of Electronic Gaming Monthly, I saw an article about the new Batman game for the Gameboy. It looked so freaking awesome. I had to have it. Unfortunately, it was months away. I came across an advertisement for import games in the same magazine and found to my surprise you could already buy the game. Back then, games came out in Japan long before they did here. The only problem was, I had 80 dollars, and after shipping and handling it was going to be over a hundred dollars. I went to my Dad and tried to get him to loan me the rest. You can sense where this is going, I'm sure.

"Hey Dad, I realllyyy want this game can you loan me the extra 20 dollars? I'll do some extra chores."

"Why don't you have the money yourself?"

"Oh, I just came up a little short, I'll make it up to you."

"That's an expensive game. A hundred bucks. You're a real top of the line kind of guy, aren't you son?"

"Uh, I guess so."

"That's great, so am I. The only difference is if I want the top of the line, I just buy it because I have the money from busting my ass. You had the opportunity to bust ass side by side with Dennis, and then you'd have money for top of the line. But you didn't. So no, I'm not going to loan you a dime."

And I never forgot it. Sometimes, you have to bust ass, big time if you want to justify getting something you want, and there is no amount of "working smart" that will get it done.

Overly Verbose.

Yes, I'm aware that I just used a moderately sized word to criticize using big or overly verbose thoughts. Look, we should all be educated. God, I wish more Americans had amazing education and would learn to use more big words and articulate them better. However, we also have a class of people for whom running their mouth incessantly is considered "smart." I can tell you; I know people that can talk for 45 minutes, and you won't retain a damn word they uttered. Or more likely, you fell asleep at the 15-minute mark. I'll tell you who was incredible at this: Barack Obama. That guy could go on and on for 45 minutes on the most basic of points, and I doubt even he remembered what he said after 5 minutes. Any good writer will tell you to learn to use fewer words. Don't say something with 40 words that you could say with 25. This especially applies to leading and public speaking as well. Don't get off topic, and don't over-explain, or you will lose your audience. If you can communicate a point in 30 seconds in an impactful manner, that's what matters.

One mistake I made often early in my career was that I valued facts far too highly. People respond far better to emotion than facts. I've talked about this topic a lot in this book, because it's fundamental to understanding how humans work, and thus gaining control over your mind. In our logical mind, we think to ourselves, "Well he uses such big words, he must be smart and well educated." That's what liberals loved about Barack Obama. Listening to him made them feel smarter. By him using big words and being far too verbose, it made them feel intelligent, even if they couldn't tell you 5% of what he just said. Compare to the language Donald Trump uses. Trump uses small, visually impactful words, in a memorable way. By doing this, they stick in your head, whether you want them to or not. Donald Trump is considered a moron by a lot of people that loved Obama because he doesn't make them feel smart. The funny part about Trump is he will accidentally use a big word once in awhile, and you can almost watch him visibly catch himself and revert to a smaller more visual word. He knows that simple, emotional communication trumps a verbose reading of the facts for 45 minutes any day of the week.

Always know that people will forget a significant amount of what you said, but they will remember how you made them feel. If you can do both, it's like a superpower. Getting people to retain virtually everything you said and put them in a positive mind frame about you and your subject matter.

That is winning.

"You only live once, but if you do it right, once is enough."

-Mae West

SECTION THREE: THE IRON LIFE

Section Three

The Iron Life

We've come a long way so far. I've gotten you to the point of changing the way you see your own life and the way you perceive things are going on around you. This perception change is paramount because, in order to apply all of the information in this chapter, you will have to bring to bear the entire armament I've provided up till now. Now, we move out of the realm of the mind, and into the real world.

Everything up till now has been setting the stage.

We've learned the degree to which the food we eat affects us; now it's time to get into diet strategy.

We've learned the benefits of working out, and how it affects our state of mind, so we will look into workouts and processes.

We also learned every trick in the book (literally) to adjust the way we perceive events and challenges, so now it's time to overcome them.

Also, we learned how to change the way we perceive ourselves and the world, which is by far the most important aspect of this book.

It's time to start Living the Iron Life.

Chapter XXX

Serenity Through Order

Take a good look around your immediate environment. How messy is it? I'm sitting here with my massive dog in my lap typing this on an iPad, and I observe my surroundings. There are a few dirty paw prints on the floor, damn it. My three bonsai trees are symmetrically lined up, as are my game consoles under the tv. Unfortunately, both the Bonsais and the various under-tv electronics do have a thin sheen of dust coating them. Damn it; now there's a big patch of dog hair up against the wall. So this room is pretty damn far from immaculate. I do have some cool decorations and art I love, all meticulously selected from things I think are cool, which I have all lined up and symmetrical. The minor weekly cleaning needs to be done, but overall, the room is laid out in a very pleasing and organized manner. It's effortless to be at my most relaxed and serene in my home. Messy spaces drive me insane, and I do all I can to keep the surrounding chaos to a minimum.

I will tell you one thing my Dad told me a long time ago, and it has never once not been correct. You can determine a tremendous amount about someone just from their car or house. Show me someone with a messy house or car, and I can guarantee their life isn't exactly in winning shape either. Ever look in someone's car, and there's like three days of McDonald's trash in the backseat? I can flat out promise you that person isn't exactly setting the world on fire. I've never known someone who really had their act together and had a great life, which had a super messy house or car. If they treat their house and car like crap, what does that say about how they execute their life? Maybe I've just described you, and you just realized you left a bacon egg and cheese wrapper in the passenger seat, or you've got a pile of clothes on the floor so deep you forgot what color your carpet is. You would be astounded the amount of information someone can extrapolate about you based on a 30-second glance over your car.

It's time to get this chaos under control. Jordan Peterson calls it "cleaning your room." I'm not saying you've got to have millimeter perfect symmetry as I like to have, but we have to get the chaos under control. Chaos breeds more chaos. Keep your workspace, car, and home at least semi-orderly. Look, I'm not going to lie, I have two pieces of clothes in the corner of my room. You don't need this perfectly immaculate area that you give the white glove treatment to every day. It just has to have some semblance of order. So get your life together and keep your areas clean, it is a reflection on the rest of your life, so while I tell you to clean up bad habits, you have to clean your spaces as well. It's all connected.

Another thing I will suggest in regards to the things you surround yourself with: Try to surround yourself with quality. Now, this doesn't mean you run out and buy Rolexes you can't afford. What it does involve is to research your purchases, and try to buy things that are trouble free and will last. I know this seems obvious, but after having been in sales for over two decades watching people purchase total disposable trash, I feel I have to say something. The objects we choose to purchase can be a massive source of stress. Buying a better quality product isn't just something you should do because you want nicer stuff, it's something you do to keep mental stress down. I'll give an example here. I use Apple products. Now I'm sure that some immediately think I'm a sheep, and probably just threw this book in the trash, but let me explain myself. I like buying things that not only serve a purpose but also don't cause me undue stress. I choose items that stay out of my way, and don't break. Here is the tally of Apple Products that I've owned:

Four iPods

Nine iPhones

Eight iPads

Six Macs

Three Apple TVs

Three Airport Extremes

One HomePod

Dozens of miscellaneous peripherals like keyboards, mice, headphones, etc.

I have owned dozens of Apple products. Are they perfect, hell no. Do they have issues that I wish Apple would fix, hell yes. But one thing I will say: They are rock fucking solid reliable. I've seen an issue here and there with Apple products; I know no piece of technology is perfect. But the overwhelming insanely high level of reliability allows me to overlook the minor annoyance here and there. And their support is superb. The point of this spiel is that I have a zillion Apple products, and they don't bring any undue stress into my life, except some minor thing once in awhile.

The point is to surround yourself with quality. Don't overspend for bullshit, but research even something as simple as a pair of pants. Find the stuff that lasts, and most importantly, removes stress from your existence.

When one is surrounded by chaos, invariably their life will become chaotic. To change your life, start by changing your environment. Order breeds order, chaos breeds chaos.

Generate serenity through order, and start by cleaning up your environments.

Chapter XXXI

The Media Addiction Vortex

We live in an age of addiction. Companies have figured out at a very high level how to stoke the dopamine production in our brains to keep us addicted to things. Whether it be games, TV, Movies, whatever it is, a significant portion of the world is completely addicted to media consumption. I am as guilty as anyone walking this earth of being sucked into the media addiction vortex. I spent YEARS of my life doing little else but consuming media. Binging out Netflix shows, going to the movies, or raiding in World of Warcraft sucked up years of my life. Now let me just say, there is nothing wrong with any of these things in isolation. Appropriately managed, they can provide tremendous stress relief and escape for a time. Unfortunately for some, myself included, they became an actual alternate reality.

For a long time in my life, I was unhappy, but I masked it by escaping into the virtual worlds that modern technology provided. When one is dissatisfied with the state of one's life, it's easy to play projection tricks as I mentioned earlier. You may have a terrible life of debt, depression, and loneliness, but you can use virtual worlds to absolve yourself of attaining solutions. I've seen people sink in the depths of despair, and use virtual worlds to make themselves forget. After all, you might be a colossal loser in real life, but these games afford you the ability to be an ultra badass in a virtual world. I remember it well when I sunk into the depths of debt and despair, but I was one of the most famous Druids on my server in World of Warcraft. My life was in tatters, but instead of addressing the underlying issues, I sunk my time into WoW and used my status in game to make myself feel better. I knew I was in trouble when I took a two-week vacation from work and didn't leave the house one single time. I spent the entirety of my vacation playing WoW 12+ hours a day. By any standard, that is a problem. Unless you can play professionally and actually make a living from it, that level of dedication is hugely problematic.

Let me talk about video games for a moment. I love games. Always have, even when being a "nerd" was the least cool thing ever. When I was growing up, I played games with no graphics on a monochrome screen. I remember the first color games, and now I play on high-end PCs and PlayStation 4s with insanely immersive graphics and mechanics. Keep in mind now; these modern games aren't just graphically and mechanically immersive, they are designed to be addictive as possible. Notice how many rewards and achievements and titles and whatnot are showered on the player constantly. That's not an accident, that's science. Every one of those little things spikes that Dopamine and keeps the player playing. I remember what I consider to be Patient Zero in this addiction era: Diablo. Diablo is a game where you control a player running around in dungeons and other areas killing demons and every single time one dies; you get some sort of reward. Now that reward might be as trivial as a few pieces of gold, but it might also be the most epic, soul-destroying weapon of all time. So Diablo was like playing slots, you would kill the same enemies over and over, hoping for that incredibly rare drop. When I say I was addicted to this game, that's not even remotely hyperbole. I played this game day in and day out, all hours of the night. Then I found World of Warcraft, which made Diablo look like aspirin by comparison to WOW's heroin.

World of Warcraft was like digital crack cocaine for me. Everything Diablo did, WOW did on a far more massive scale. In Diablo the addiction was apparent, you killed guys, and they dropped loot, hopefully, something impressive. It was simple. WOW took that to entirely higher level. It had achievements, reputations, and all different manner of loot. Then WOW also added raids that required anywhere from 10-40 players. So, you'd kill a boss character, and he'd drop the most insanely rare stuff to spread amongst other people with whom you ran. So there was a whole extra layer of addictions in the framework of WOW. I was planted in front of WOW all day, every day for a very long time. Then on top of that, I raided every single night. I was, at one point, raiding seven nights a week. That's how all-consuming this was for me. Now, as addicted as I was, nothing compares to how addicted my friend Shawn was. Before WOW there were two predecessors, Everquest and Ultima Online. Once he started playing these games, I never saw Shawn. Every once in awhile, I'd swing by his house to see if he was still alive. Once I went to his apartment, and he had pizza crust lying on the floor. He had the side of his computer open, and a McDonald's fry box inside of it, overflowing with cigarette ashes. Another time during his Everquest days, I went to his house, and he had two-liter bottles full of urine in his room. Mold grew all over his bathroom. I really wish I was making this up.

I still enjoy games and play them a lot. However, I don't allow them to dominate my being the way I did in the past. I've spent a lot of time trashing World of Warcraft and some of these video games. Let me be clear; I still love games. I also love a fantastic TV show or movie. However, there comes the point where you have to check yourself to see if you are more plugged into virtual worlds than real ones. These escapes have to be appropriately managed. The games particularly can easily take years off your life, as I can attest to World of Warcraft doing just that. Let me tell you how this works. If you have played a modern video game for even 5 minutes, you will know exactly what I'm talking about here. So get ready, here's the addiction process for every game on the planet nowadays:

1. Open up game.
2. You are showered with eye-catching and pleasing effects and music.
3. You take literally any action in the game.
4. You are immediately showered with some spectacular reward.
5. Your brain gets a nice little dopamine kick.
6. Play for another minute and you are showered with some other reward or achievement.
7. The brain gets dopamine kick.
8. Play a little longer and get an even more massive spectacular reward.
9. Dopamine Kick.
10. Rinse and repeat ad infinitum.

In the initial stages of a game, you are showered with rewards every two minutes to get you addicted to the kick of dopamine from pleasing accomplishments. As the game progresses, the rewards space out a bit more and become more challenging to get, ironically making them more pleasing due to the level of difficulty. Towards the end of my World of Warcraft career, I had raided for thousands of hours for even an infinitesimal chance to receive a piece of rare gear. I look back at my career in the game, and I certainly enjoyed it, but I gained nothing of value. In the thousands of hours spent playing that game, I could have learned multiple languages, any number of trades or skills that would have advanced my real life, not my virtual one. I had fun a lot of the time, but I took it to a level that was just too much, unless I planned on playing professionally, which I was nowhere near good enough to do.

If you want proof of how completely and utterly companies have refined this dopamine reward system, look no further than the ultimate example of brain hijacking: Idle Tappers. Idle Tappers are an entire class of games that have no gameplay, other than tapping the screen as fast as you can. No decision making, no strategy, nothing. The entirety of the game is tapping the screen and being showered with rewards and pretty colors. I played one of these, and I'm here to tell you, it's like they distilled the addiction mechanisms of WoW and Diablo down to their purest form: perform an action, be showered in rewards. Why bother with all the strategy when you can just get straight to the dopamine kick just by tapping the screen? I played one of these for nearly an hour, and I can tell you, I swear I felt brain cells eroding during play. I literally felt dumber after an hour of this game.

Movies and TV are the same, but I'd argue not nearly as addictive. Companies have gotten exceedingly good at managing addiction. Let me give you the exact layout of virtually every network tv show ever, which you will immediately recognize as soon as I say it:

1. 2-5 Minutes of character development.
2. Introduce conflict.
3. Spend 20 minutes resolving.
4. At precisely the 30 minute mark introduce a plot twist.
5. Make a revelation before every commercial.
6. Within the last 5 minutes, another plot twist.
7. 2 minutes of character development.

I dare you to watch virtually any network TV show and watch it follow that pattern exactly. Make no mistake, these companies have become experts at addiction and learning when to spike dopamine to keep you engaged.

The point of all of this to get you to understand that these things need regulation. The saying goes, all things in moderation. That's true except for one thing: forging an iron mind. In that, we don't want moderation.

We want to dominate.

Chapter XXXII

Monetize Your Life

To develop the Iron Mind, we have to reduce stress. A lot of the techniques I've introduced are designed to do just that. And let me tell you, it is tough to overcome stress under financial strain. Being in debt is like having a massive anvil hanging over your head, ready to drop and crush you at any moment. I've had to learn a lot of hard lessons financially. I've been on the verge of bankruptcy and total ruin a few times now, so I know how this feels. It's a terrible feeling to be independent, and then have to move back into your parent's house because you let your finances get out of control. On the other hand, when I was 18, I couldn't wait to get out of the house, yet nowadays young people are far more likely to stay in their parent's house until they are 26. That would have been unthinkable to me when I graduated in 1995. Now, kids are content to stay at home indefinitely and buy parts for their car or computer with their money.

The first thing you have to realize is: Money is stress until you have enough for it not to matter. It's that simple. Every dollar you spend that you can't afford is just adding to a little stress meter inside your head. Think of it as a life meter in a video game, only instead of going down, it goes up. It starts out in the green, for little stress, then escalates into the yellow and finally the red for maximum stress. I've been in the far red section of that bar multiple times and managed to drag myself out. As I write this, my stress is in the green. I'm relaxed, confident, and generally stress-free. When I used to buy things

I couldn't afford, I did it to feel good in the moment, which is far easier to do than processing bad feelings you are trying to erase by buying something. I've been in sales my whole life, and I've seen people drain their bank account dry to have something they absolutely didn't need.

The reason I'm writing this chapter is that work and finances are beyond critical to having the Iron Mind. It is very, very difficult to have an Iron Mind and be drowning in debt at a job you hate. You have to understand that those things feed your negative mind frame, and thus, have to be changed to improve. We learned to reframe in previous chapters, but it has its limits. Both of the times I was near bankrupt and in massive debt, I had to change jobs. This seems like the most obvious thing in the world, but it can be very tough. Even a job you like might have to be on the chopping block if it isn't paying the bills. I've had to quit jobs I enjoyed, because I was comfortable. Comfort and complacency are dangerous things that can get you into all kinds of trouble. Sometimes you have to recognize it's time to make a change and do it. If your financial situation is untenable, you have to make a plan to either move on or move up. It is that simple. Do not allow comfort and friends to dictate otherwise.

I've been there. Tens of thousands in debt at a job I hate. So what did I do? I made a plan to get out. First up, get a promotion. I didn't like the job that much, but I knew I had to make myself more valuable down the road to other businesses. I then took a promotion I didn't actually want, just to buff up my resume and get a tiny raise. I've done this more than once, and sometimes you have to take a short-term bullet to play the long game of getting out of debt and into something you want to do. The second thing I did was to consolidate my bills. I had multiple maxed credit cards and couldn't even afford to cover the interest. If you get in that situation, move to get out immediately. Consolidation brought me to one manageable payment and crushed the insane amount of interest I was paying each month. The third thing is: get better at everything. Every new skill you add, every certification you get, just makes you more valuable down the road. Scott Adams calls it a skill stack. It's also known as being a polymath, or someone who has become great at multiple disciplines. The better you get at multiple skills, the more likely you are to find someone that needs one of those skills. So, when you are implementing this plan, take on every challenge you can. If a job offers other certifications or opportunities, do it. In a letter to the leader of Milan, Leonardo da Vinci spent considerable time selling his engineering skill to get a job, and at the very end included the line "Likewise with painting, I can do everything possible." As one of the foremost polymaths in all of history, he understood having connecting skills, and skills that intersected was incredibly valuable. We also see in that quote incredible confidence in his skill set. You might not be Leonardo, but understand that there is time enough in your life to master an incredibly broad range of skills that make you very valuable.

The advantage to the skill stack is that you don't even have to be world class amazing at any one thing. If you take enough skills combined with the will to power, you can achieve greatness even with mediocre talent. Take a look at Kobe Bryant, Leonardo da Vinci, Donald Trump, and Michael Jordan. These are all examples of people who didn't have one dominating characteristic or talent, other than dominating willpower. They combine multiple excellent skills with the will to power, and they dominate. Any chance you have to build your skill stack, do it. It doesn't even matter what it is, add it. My dad is a fabulous example of a monster skill stack. He was expert level in so many areas it's hard to comprehend. He could literally build a house, car, or computer from ground zero. Anything that even remotely resembled any building he could do. Even now I find it impressive how many disciplines he was able to master, without the use of the internet. His skill stack was so broad and all-encompassing that he could get any number of jobs he wanted. I'm sure some would say that's just half-assing a lot of things instead of becoming super great at one thing. First, most of us don't have a ridiculous talent for one thing. Myself, for example, I don't have any one overarching talent. Let's take a look at my skill stack.

1. Public Speaking
2. Computer Hardware
3. Photo and Video editing
4. Presentation Skills
5. Writing (I hope you agree at least)
6. Design and Typography
7. Sales Skills
8. Vocabulary
9. Can withstand criticism
10. Physical fitness knowledge and practice.
11. Nutritional education and practice.
12. Business Management

Now, I don't profess to be the greatest at any of those, and I'm not here for self-aggrandizement. However, that's a pretty solid stack that can allow me to do many different things. This is part of the operating system mentality you should have for your mind. When you look at your mind as computer software that can have new programs installed, it increases the functionality. Think of it, imagine if you bought a computer, and it only had the best email client of all time installed. No photo, video, word processing, calendar, note or internet software. For those of us with no discernible top talent, we have to rely on will and getting really good at a lot of things.

Back to finances. When you get an opportunity with your job to take stock options and a 401K, do it immediately. I left a ton of money on the table by waiting to do this. Now, at the time I still had some debt to pay off, so I let those things slide until I had my debt paid off, but I took longer doing so when I could just as easily paid off the debt several months later. Another thing: abuse the hell out of reward points. This requires tremendous discipline, because it means you need to use a credit card for everything, and pay it off EVERY month. In the end however, it is worth it. I pull in the thousands of dollars in free money just by running everything through a credit card and making absolutely sure to pay it off. If you can get this routine going, it will make a tremendous difference. Get the absolute best point ratio for daily purchases you can, and light it up on everything you buy each month. By the end of the year, you will have amassed hundreds if not thousands of dollars in reward points. Use every available reward card as well, and you will rake in the cash. Just don't be stupid and do it for things you can't afford. It's critical to pay it off every month, or it blows the entire point away.

Keep your finances in line; your stress level will thank you for it.

Chapter XXXIII

Immunity of the Gods

Eat food off the floor.

Lick dollar bills.

Don't wash your hands.

These are just a few of the utterly ludicrous things I tell people I do. I don't actually do any of those things really, but I say it to make a point. I am almost never sick. Sitting here typing this right now, I honestly couldn't tell you when the last time it was that I was ill. My immune system has been essentially bulletproof for decades now, and so I looked into it to find out why some get sick a lot, and some not at all.

> *"The right raw materials can double or triple the protective power of the immune system."*
>
> *-Joel Fuhrman*

There's a guy I used to work with; let's call him Mike. Mike is constantly sick. I'm mean this guy is legitimately sick at least once a month. He misses work and comes in so regularly sick that it's a running joke. The interesting thing about Mike is that he goes so far out of his way to avoid germs. He's the type of guy that doesn't want to touch the bathroom door, who washes his hands for like 5 minutes at a time. He uses insane amounts of hand sanitizer as well. He does everything possible to dodge germs, and yet somehow is regularly sick. I contrast that with myself. I am never sick, and yet I do all kinds of "gross" stuff. I hardly ever wash my hands unless something visible on them. I don't mind picking a piece of food I just dropped on the floor and eating it. Basically, the gist of it all is that I don't pay even the slightest attention to germs. I tell people all the time my immune system has a bunch of little commandoes in there running around machine-gunning viruses to death.

The point is, like a lot of things I mention in this book, you have a higher degree of control than you might think. As I discussed earlier, so much of our lives, body, and mind are interconnected. All of the following have a significant impact on how often we get sick:

1. Getting enough Sleep[1].
2. Proper nutrients through diet and supplements.
3. Stress levels.
4. Working out and fitness.
5. Interacting with people.
6. Not Laughing enough.
7. Allowing your immune system to adapt.

Any one of those can create the conditions necessary for you get sick. When I look through that list, I meet all of the criteria. Thus I've created an environment that is conducive to not being sick. Now let's take my friend Mike. Mike stays up all hours of the night gaming and virtually never gets proper sleep. He doesn't work out, nor does he have a proper diet. He

---

[1] https://www.webmd.com/sleep-disorders/features/immune-system-lack-of-sleep

does do 5 and 6, as his job involves him interacting with a lot of people and he has a good sense of humor, so neither of those are a problem. So basically, it boils down to 1-4 and 7. In other words, he's likely to be sick often because he's fulfilled a lot of the criteria that contribute to creating an environment in the body that is likely to have a weak defense. The reason I bring this up is that it's harder to maintain the iron mind while sick. In my powerlifting days, I hated being sick because it took me out of my game. I don't care what kind of willpower you have, being deathly ill is going to compromise work, play, and any sort of progress you might want to make in life. So, we have to make a concerted effort not to be sick. Now, I'd argue doing the things on the above list are beneficial independent of keeping you from getting sick. I've discussed them all at length in this book for their benefits in building the iron mind or developing into the person you want to be.

So let's take a look at number 7 on that list. This is the questionable one. The others are widespread processes for increasing well-being. Number 7 is a theory I've had for a long time, that I only recently saw backed up by science[2]. Basically, in evaluating my life to determine why it is I don't get sick, I noticed something I've been doing for decades. Or not doing. Not caring about bacteria. This is backed up by science, but I can't entirely prove that the actions I've been taking for decades have increased my immunity to various illnesses. While others slathered themselves in hand sanitizer,

---

[2] https://www.nih.gov/news-events/nih-research-matters/immune-system-shaped-environment-more-genes

I don't think I've ever used it once. In other words, allowing my immune system to handle whatever germs are thrown at me as opposed to externally trying to control interacting with bacteria, I believe has given me a monster immune system. Now, again, I've been brutally sick before, it's not as if I never get sick, but it is sporadic. Besides generally eating clean and working out, I'd say by far the most significant contributor is that I allowed my immune system to handle its business and do what it's supposed to do. It stands to reason that if your immune system doesn't develop through being exposed to bacteria, it will get crushed the minute it gets hit with some new strain.

I'll put it to you this way: I always ask myself before I do something "unclean" or "unsanitary" the following question:

Is this going to kill me or give me an incurable disease? If the answer is no, then I don't care about it. So what if something you touched had some germs? Are you going to die from it? If not, then stop sweating it.

Remember: The body adapts. It adapts to everything. It adapts to eating, workload, and indeed bacteria. Developing an Iron Immune system goes hand in hand with the Iron Mind.

Ditch the hand sanitizer. Make your immune system earn a living.

So I just spent the entirety of this chapter bragging about how ridiculously bulletproof my immune system is and how I never get sick. Obviously, there's some hyperbole in there, as anyone is going to get sick at some point. So what do you do when you do get sick? What is the best way to knock it out quickly? Clearly, it's going to depend on what the problem is, but I'm here to tell you there is something borderline magical you can do:

Drink Tea.

Obviously, I'm not talking about the sweetened tea you got from Chic-Fil-A. I'm talking hardcore hot herbal teas. I have yet to find any medicine or treatment as effective as tea at laying waste to various illnesses. If you go to Amazon or the grocery store, there are a million different teas, for treatment of virtually anything. You can brew up a tea in two minutes flat to address nearly any basic sickness. So, I get sick I start pounding tea. Now, I drink a lot of tea in the colder months regardless, which probably helps. However, the minute I start feeling any sickness, whether its Sinus, digestive, Sore Throat, Cold or Flu, I begin going berserk on the tea. Also, you are staying hydrated on top of providing all the herbs to try to knock out your sickness. Then, on top of all that, tea is absurdly cheap. You get boxes on top of boxes for next to nothing, literally pennies per teabag. So stock up on tea, and if you feel something coming on, or you just want to play a prevent defense, drink a lot of tea.

So then what else do we do when we get sick? Besides pounding ridiculous amounts of tea? Well, the first thing we do is not act like a pathetic weenie. We still show up to work, and we still do what we have to and not lay in bed like a lazy scrub. I can count on one hand the number of times I've ever called in sick, and only a couple were due to a violent illness. My bosses always understood one thing: They could rely on me, no matter what. And that makes you valuable. They knew if I called out from work, I must be damn near dead. I see people all the time calling out for sickness, every other week. That's absurd. All that does is teach people that you can't be counted on when it's needed. Calling out every other week gets you a reputation, and you better pray to god you never try for a promotion or need something, because they will laugh in your face if you've been unreliable. No boss I have ever had has ever had the temerity to deny me anything, you know why? Because I was a top performer who never, ever, called out sick, and was always on time. I once had a boss buy a new engine for my car when it broke down. She gave me 1,500 dollars to get a new engine for my car. You do not get that sort of generosity if you have anything short of ironclad reliability. If you can do that, people will worship you, and coworkers will wonder why bosses always seem to give you the benefit of the doubt.

Get sick = Go to work, drink tea, and be tough, unless it's really awful.

Chapter XXXIV

The Fairness Doctrine

Let me tell you what you deserve in this world:

Absolutely nothing.

Every single time I see some commercial on TV telling people how special they are, and how there's only one of you, and you deserve the world, I just roll my eyes. You deserve nothing in this life; you have to take it and become what you are capable of. Do you know what the lowest bar possible on this planet is?

Procreation.

Even cockroaches procreate. You aren't special because someone birthed you, or you birthed someone else. Your ancestors toiled relentlessly because they knew they didn't deserve anything, they had to make it or take it. Do you believe that any neanderthal running around with a stone-tipped spear thought the world owed him anything? Of course not. Nowadays, we live in a privileged world. Everyone seems to think they are owed everything, whether it's healthcare, internet, or worse, a partner. I think it's hilarious to listen to both genders tell themselves how much they deserve an amazing partner.

You deserve nothing. I can't count the number of people I've known with the following list of attributes which couldn't figure out why they were single:

1. Overweight or out of shape.
2. Awful personality, either shy or a jerk.
3. Terrible Job.
4. No ambition.
5. Sits inside to play video games all day.
6. Dresses terribly.
7. No effort into hair or appearance.

Setting all of that aside, maybe you do have something going for you but understand this, I don't care how much you work out, or how good of a job you have, or how much your friends toot your horn, the world doesn't owe you a damn thing. Oh, you thought because you got in shape that all of a sudden the hottest women or men are all of a sudden just going to materialize into your life? Wrong. Everything in life has to be earned. If you want a great job, you have to build the skills to make yourself invaluable, and learn to present yourself in a manner that would make them foolish not to hire you. If you want to find a significant other to marry, then you have to make yourself marriage material, and go out and find someone to marry.

Life isn't fair, in any way, shape, or form, and it isn't ever going to be.

> *"The world isn't fair Calvin." "I know, but why isn't it ever unfair in my favor?"*
>
> *-Bill Watterson, Calvin and Hobbes*

You hear this a lot. "Life isn't fair" is a line that's been thrown around forever, that we hear once in awhile and give little thought to as we cry our way through whatever thing is afflicting us at the moment. Worrying about how fair or unfair something is will get you precisely nowhere. Stop and think for a moment. How many times have you thought about something someone had that you just knew they didn't deserve? Maybe someone was born into wealth and has just had it easier than you, maybe someone else has a bigger penis, or breasts if you are self-conscious about your body image.

This fairness issue is one reason young people are overwhelmingly liberal, and in this day and age, quite a few are actually communists. The root of all of this younger person mentality is fairness. They just can't stand the fact that someone has more than someone else. It's so unfair that some kids are born into poverty while some rich guy flies all over the world in his private jet. I'm going to be honest, I have certainly been guilty of this. You know what used to drive me nuts?

Genetics.

It used to make me borderline insane that some people were born with better genetics. In my powerlifting days, there were people everywhere that didn't train anywhere near as hard as I did, and were bigger, stronger, had better joints, the works. It took me a lot of years to come to terms with the fact that I just had poor genetics for lifting. Even when I was 18 years old, I had to wear knee braces to play basketball, and during my lifting, I was always afflicted with various joint, ligament, and muscular injuries. I'd see guys twice as big as me come into the gym, lazily swing around a couple of weights while chatting to everyone in sight. Meanwhile, I'm over here murdering myself every day and giving every ounce of my soul. How is that fair? It isn't. Because life isn't. The cards we are dealt is the hand we have to play. It took me a long time, but I got over it. Part of how I got over it was just pushing myself to the breaking point every day. So now, I have nothing to prove. I will train right next to the biggest toughest guy in the building, because I know deep down I gave it everything I had. And that's enough. As long as you know, inside, that you gave it your all, that's what matters. Never leave anything on the table to look back on and regret.

You know what else isn't fair? Acquisition of stuff. The absurd irony of being rich is that once you have money, it becomes far easier to acquire more of it. Having exceptional credit is another one. Once you have it, it becomes far easier to get more of it. Now, of course, it's possible to lose everything, but you have to get absurdly stupid to pull that off. If you even remotely manage investments and credit even sort of correctly, it is so easy to build on an existing fortune. So let's go back to the rich guy hate from earlier. The guy that all the communist kids can't stand. Kids look at these things superficially. They see a guy who is uber-wealthy and think to themselves, "capitalism is bullshit, wealth should be distributed fairly!" The problem with that statement is that they just don't have the perspective or knowledge to understand that they don't see the whole picture. What they don't seem to understand about "fairness" is that no one can agree what fair is. What is your fair share of someone else's money? Who is going to enforce this "fairness" of yours anyway? This is also why left wing people are obsessed with gender. They cannot stand the fact that there is any difference in people. I'm not sure what fantasy land people are living in, but there are always going to be differences in human beings.

Some will be stronger, smarter, better looking. The one thing you can control that can tilt the balance of power is the effort. You might have been born without "fair" attributes, but you can control the level of effort you produce.

One of the funniest instances of lack of fairness I've ever seen was when Donald Trump's doctor was getting grilled over his physical and mental state. Remember when the reporter incredulously asked him this:

"How does he drink Diet Coke, eat Mcdonalds and KFC constantly, and still be as healthy as you say he is without working out?"

"Genetics."

That's just reality. There's going to be people out there, even people you hate, that just won the life lottery. Do not spend a moment hating or wishing. Reframe instantly. You've got bigger things to worry about than what Donald Trump can eat for breakfast every day and not die. The other interesting piece that came out of the Doctor's press conference was in his words:

"The president just has the uncanny ability to reset every day. Nothing seems to get to him."

Doubt will assail you. You will have bad days. Everyone does. A tremendous strength is how quickly you can reset. It's how guys like Michael Jordan can miss ten shots in a row but have ultimate confidence taking the 11th. Being able to reset after a setback or even just daily is a fantastic ability. Learn to go to bed, and treat it as a total erasure of the day. Waking up to new possibilities every single day.

Worry about yourself, and seek to imbalance the world in your favor. Make other people feel that it isn't fair to compete against you.

The Fairness Doctrine is that the world owes you nothing. You deserve nothing.

Now go take it.

Chapter XXXV

Drama-Free Dating

Why do I include romantic relationships in a book about developing the Iron Mind? Because so many people make a lot of mental errors in relationships that contribute to stress, which degrade our overall mind frame. Relationships are a massive part of our lives. They can add an enormous amount of tension and mental weight to our lives. They can singlehandedly ruin lives, or advance us to a higher level of happiness. The key is to manage them correctly. Men especially make a lot of mistakes that are easily corrected, an immense trove of simple things that can enhance your happiness, but also that of your partner. One thing I look back on and can say for sure that's made my life better is the way I've managed romantic relationships in my life. I have zero drama in my life as a result of the relationships in my life. A lot of these tips are things I didn't know were beneficial while I was doing them, much like most of the other elements in this book. Over the course of years I realized I was doing things organically that would benefit my mind frame long term. Learning to manage the romantic relationships in your life will contribute to either making or breaking your chances for success in building an Iron Mind.

I will write this from a male perspective, but I will endeavor to include information that will be beneficial for both genders. The first and foremost thing you absolutely must understand in relationships:

Logic and Facts will get you nowhere.

If you believe you are going to get anywhere with the opposite sex using logic and facts, you are relegating yourself to having a rough time in relationships. I would argue this is definitely true even outside of romantic relationships, but it is beyond critical that you understand this point in the context of romantic relationships. We as humans like to believe that we rationally evaluate all the facts, and then come to a reasonable decision. In reality, any decision that has an emotional component we make decisions using confirmation bias and emotion, then rationalize that decision. How many times have you had a heated disagreement with the opposite sex, in a situation where you knew you were right? I already know the answer to this, and it happens all the time. Men especially try so hard to be logical when in an argument with a significant other, only to find that the harder they work, the worse it gets.

Ask any man if they have ever argued with a significant other. The answer is of course, yes. Ask them how many times the argument escalated to a fight, despite the fact they were right in their initial assertion. This happens a lot because men overwhelming try to base their argument on perceived reason and logic. Women especially want you to understand their emotional point, not their logical point. If you try to argue logically with a woman, it will likely escalate if you don't understand the emotional substance of the disagreement. Men overwhelmingly are fixers, in that they want to know what the problem is, and try to help fix it. The problem is, women want men to understand the emotional component and support them, not dive right into trying to fix things.

That brings us to another problem: Concession. Men hate to argue so much, that they will start to concede even when they know they are right. Men generally want little to no drama in a relationship, so they do everything they can to avoid a fight. The twisted irony to this is that women aren't attracted to men who cave and don't stand up for themselves. Men then find themselves in the position of not wanting to fight, so they supplicate to the woman, thus reducing the woman's attraction to him. Very few women want a doormat, so if you become one, there is a significant likelihood that it will cause damage long-term in a relationship. I know guys that supplicate to every demand a woman makes, just praying that will get her to have sex with him. This is absolutely the wrong move. So what is the solution? If you are a man, you cannot back down if you know you're right, so you have to disagree. The trick is to have the appropriate technique to disagree.

Whatever your significant other is arguing with you about, you have to understand the emotional substance of their argument. For example, everyone has debated about where to go to eat. I once argued with a significant other after I suggested we eat at Subway. The argument spiraled out of control and ended up being a fight. I just couldn't understand at the time why this was such a big deal. The problem wasn't that I wanted to go to Subway, the problem was that I didn't understand from her perspective that she wanted to go somewhere nice to spend time with me. The Subway suggestion, to her, was a metaphor about what I thought of the quality of our relationship and how much I cared about it. This is why learning to understand the emotional content of what your partner is saying is critical. If you just operate on facts you are going to be in a lot of fights.

I am going to boil this down as clearly as I can. One simple rule, if both parties follow, will enhance things greatly and make for a much stronger relationship:

Act like you care, at all times.

One of my favorite movies is Boiler Room. If you've ever been in sales, this might be the best sales related movie of all time. In this movie, Ben Affleck makes a speech to his junior stockbrokers. In this speech he says the following:

"There's an important phrase that we use here, and think it's time that you all learned it. Act as if. You understand what that means? Act as if you are the fucking President of this firm. Act as if you got a 9" cock. Okay? Act as if."

In this context, minus the vulgarity, you have to Act as if. Act as if your significant other is the most important goddamn thing in the world. Now, this is an important quote for other aspects of the Iron Mind as well, which we will cover later. For now, though, that's the nuts and bolts of it all and encompasses numerous things both large and small. If you do that one thing, it will certainly change the game for you both. Relationships require effort, and the tiniest acknowledgment that you care can make a world of difference. For men, acting like you care means listening, not to just the words, but the emotional content of what is being said. Understand why she has the problem she does, even if to you it doesn't add up in your logical mind. Understanding that small gestures, such as notes or flowers make a big difference because they show that you care. If you leave her a nice note, she doesn't care in the least about the note itself; she cares that you took the time and thought to write it. Act as if means doing it even when you don't feel like it. The more disconnected you act, the more the relationship will suffer. Now, acting as if doesn't mean continually buying approval. It can be as simple as a small touch or gesture.

Setting expectations up front.

I cannot stress this enough. This gets so many people into trouble, including me back in the day. This is why the beginning stages and later stages of relationships can be truly different because you both likely presented glossed over versions of yourself that you thought would be appealing to the other person. Everyone does it, and it is tough to exhibit the real version of yourself up front to someone you like. This requires tremendous courage because sometimes the real version of yourself doesn't have the most appealing traits. However, you spare yourself an enormous amount of time, money, and anguish if you are up front. This requires a tough look at yourself, and what you need out of a relationship. If the other person is incapable of providing a core necessity, then you are in the wrong relationship. Compromise is one thing, settling for something that's outside of what you know is something you have to have is a huge mistake. If you don't set the right expectation up front, then try to come in with it later, it makes you look weak, and catches the other person off guard, thus likely resulting in a fight.

I'll give one example. I have a friend who has a massive sex drive. It is impossible for him to be happy in a relationship that doesn't involve a lot of sex. He told his then-girlfriend up front that lots of sex was a non-negotiable component of a happy relationship. This took a lot of balls and goes against today's logic, but he did it anyway. He's been with his wife for over ten years now, has a child, and happy life. The key to the whole thing was setting the expectation that this was one thing he would need to be happy, and told her, rather than have her find out later since this was a core issue for him. If there is something you know that you need, whether it be sex, alone time, dogs, whatever, the best thing you can do is get it out there as quickly as possible. Setting the right expectations both in life, work, and relationships makes a tremendous difference in results and happiness. Another prime example is religion. I've seen nonreligious people try to have a relationship with someone overly religious. Is it possible? Of course, but not likely. I have quite literally seen atheists go church in the initial stages of a relationship just to try to appeal to the other person. That is a terrible idea. Religion is such a core belief that in and of itself can be a deal breaker. If you aren't going to go all in, then you might want to move on to someone more compatible.

In my own life, I have a few examples, but I'll share one here. I used to do a lot of powerlifting and bodybuilding. I lived and breathed it for years, to the point of ignoring relationships to a large degree. At one point, I did meet a girl, and I set the expectation up front that nothing in our relationship would interfere with my gym time. She was fine with it, so she was never surprised when I couldn't stay out late or do something that compromised my workouts. She was fine with it because I let her know up front this was the way it was going to be. Now, had I not said anything and set that expectation, the first time I didn't want to stay over because I had to work out in the morning, she would have been up all night wondering about the state of our relationship. Because she already knew, it wasn't a big deal, and would occasionally even go with me. As the Joker said in the Dark Knight: "No one is surprised when things go according to plan, even if the plan is horrifying."

Speaking of deal breakers, I'll share mine, because they have been really good at keeping me out of trouble and free of drama. I classify them into hard and soft deal breakers. Hard means it's an instant, no discussion, no chance killer. Soft means I can live with it, but if there's more than three, they become a hard dealbreaker. I particularly love this system, because no one is perfect, and it takes that into account. You will find that yours might be completely different from mine, because what's a hard dealbreaker for me, you may not care about in the least. You will find if you make a list like this for yourself, that even if you don't set the soft dealbreaker to 3, you'll find that right around three is when you start getting annoyed at the person. So after a lot of dates, I found setting the soft limit to 3 is a sweet spot.

Yours may vary but here's mine.

Hard Deal Breakers:

Obesity (More than 20 pounds overweight is a non-starter)

Addictions and Disease

Lack of sex drive

Soft Deal Breakers:

Super religious

Distance, or lives more than an hour away

Cleanliness

Already has kids

Parties too much

Liberal

Poor communication

Significant age difference

So there you have it. You might look at that and say I'm looking for perfection, or that I'm too picky. Well, I have news for you, being picky is what keeps you happy and drama free. Settling for mediocrity is a path to despair. In some ways, I view compromise as a dirty word. It's one thing to compromise on where to eat, or where to move the sofa to, it's entirely another thing to compromise on core beliefs. Of course, it's possible to fall for someone that meets none of my criteria, but it is highly unlikely. You could almost make an algorithm out of my taste preferences. The point of it though is to find someone that I will be compatible with long-term, and add value to my life and mind frame. I've made mistakes and added a lot of stress to my life unnecessarily, as I'm sure you have as well. What you have to do is take a hard look at your life and what makes you happy, and look for a partner that's going to fill in the gaps in your life and enhance your strengths.

So how does one go about finding someone like that? The best way is to go to places that are most likely to have the type of person that meets your needs and has the characteristics you are looking for. For example, do you want a hardcore traditionalist that wants to get married and have a bunch of kids? Hard to beat church for that. What about a highly intellectual introvert? Book clubs or the library. What about the super active traveler who is in shape? The gym or 5k running events. The point is, go where you will meet the type of person you are looking for. You probably don't want to be hanging out at a club or bar trying to find a hyper-traditionalist for example.

Another point that I cannot stress enough: Never, ever, date on potential. Potential is a dirty word to me. If they aren't what you want now, and you go in thinking you are going to change them, or make them into your perfect little soul-mate, I have got news for you; you are preparing to fail. Taking on a project is a recipe for disaster. If you have done everything you can to develop yourself into a worthy mate for someone, the worst thing you can do is settle for mediocrity in them.

Entire books have been written on this topic, so I won't belabor the point. You have to understand how significant of a pillar of your happiness relationships are, and how they can either enrich your life or crush it. Do what's necessary to keep your mind frame solid.

Chapter XXXVI

The Iron Lungs

I talked a bit in the Rituals chapter about breathing, and how it's helped me. I feel that I need to expand on that as I didn't give it enough credit, so much so that it deserves its own section. I remember when Apple came out with the breathing alert on the Apple Watch 2 Operating system, I laughed and thought man, what a foolish addition, who needs to monitor breathing on that level? I was wrong, and I'm here to tell you about how breathing can be a massive game changer in a lot of areas, and you need to learn how to do it properly. I first became acquainted with breathing practices after watching a guy named Wim Hof on Joe Rogan's podcast. I'd recommend watching it, but the gist of it is this: You can quite literally alter your body chemistry and solve a lot of problems by learning new breathing techniques. Now, initially this all sounded like a bunch of spiritualist mumbo-jumbo to me. It also didn't help that Wim Hof is an eccentric guy. He looks quite nutty and sounds it as well. So my confirmation bias was a little primed to tell me this guy is full of it.

However, results don't lie. Wim Hof has so many world records it's insane. Virtually anything related to ice or cold, he dominates. This is a guy that scaled Mount Kilimanjaro in shorts and can stay underwater in the cold for absurd amounts of time. He has his methods, and there's a lot of people that swear by them. Now back to my original point, how important is breathing? No matter what problem you have, whether it's stamina for running, lifting, sex or anything related to self-control, you can find an article somewhere that references breathing technique. I used to blow this stuff off. No way could just taking air into my lungs as I usually do in a slightly different way possibly make this kind of a difference.

Boy was I wrong.

This is a huge game changer. You can quite literally change your entire mind frame and become stronger, more calm, and happier just by learning breathing technique. Obviously, oxygen is critical to life, but people don't understand how differing intake matters to the brain and the body. Properly controlling breathing allows us to regulate the oxygen flow to the brain and blood. If you do not get the proper oxygen, it allows for a buildup of carbon dioxide, leading to oxidative stress and inflammation.[1] Do not underestimate what I say here. I cannot recommend this highly enough. Take what I talked about in the Rituals chapter:

The 4-7-8 Method

Inhale for 4 seconds.

Hold for 7 seconds.

Exhale for 8 seconds.

This sounds absurdly simple, but I'm telling you, it works. First, it redirects your mind. If you are angry, or tired, or whatever, focusing on the counting and breaths refocuses the

---

[1] http://1vigor.com/article/breathing-rhythm-technique-health/

mind. It will recenter you a bit and calm you down as you count. I used to struggle with my breathing in the gym and would hold my breath too long and take ragged gulps periodically. Now, my breathing is methodical, precise, and it allows me to continue far past what I used to do, just on the basis of airflow alone. There's a lot of different breathing techniques, but they all share one thing in common: They all work to some degree. It's mostly the same with diets and workouts. As long as you are doing it, it's helping. Not everyone needs to climb Everest, swim under ice water, or deadlift 1000 pounds. The point is, this is something I advocate, and highly recommend you add to your daily routine. When you are tired or stressed, do the above exercise, or develop your own. Use the simple one I provided, look into the Wim Hof method or other meditative breathing exercises. The point is to do it.

It will help, mark my words.

Chapter XXXVII

The Iron Body

"The greatest gift I ever gave myself was the gift of iron."

-Me

It took me a long time to decide to start working out. I was so tired of feeling terrible and inferior. I remember trying to dodge my reflection in the mirror, because I was total mush, with virtually no muscle development. I wasn't that obese by today's standards, but I felt awful constantly. Today, people seem to regard being obese as some badge of honor, saying, "Look how much I love myself, I don't even care if I'm fat," Even going so far as to create "body positive" movements trying to convince themselves and their little echo chamber online that they aren't miserable. Deep down, they all know the truth. They can hide it in the funny angles they use to take selfies and photos, but they know. I had one girl I dated send me at least 50 pictures, and upon meeting her learned she was easily 400 pounds. Some have gotten to be professionals at disguising their photographs. The truth is, they know. They know they are miserable, but try to convince themselves otherwise.

You see, you can't have the Iron Mind if you haven't earned it. Just telling yourself things you know aren't true doesn't work. The techniques I outlined earlier only work if you put in the effort. Telling yourself how awesome you are doesn't mean a thing if you do it while laying on the couch eating Doritos. The Iron Mind requires physicality; it needs to be pushed, to achieve what you want out of life. I'm not saying you have to be a bodybuilder or triathlete, but you can't be completely inactive. Have you ever noticed how many Fortune 500 CEOs are obese? Not many. There are a few, but by and large, they are at least in semi-decent shape. As I mentioned earlier, the body and mind are connected. They are symbiotic in the sense that it's very unusual to have one be great without the other. There are notable exceptions, such as Stephen Hawking and the like. The exceptional savants. Most of us aren't savants or Fortune 500 CEOs. For most of us, we need to bolster both body and mind to forge the best version of ourselves.

I've said a lot of things that go against popular convention these days, and I'm about to say another. The type of workout almost doesn't matter. That's right; we've all heard the magic promises of infomercials such as: "This workout will get you shredded in 5 minutes a day!" Or "Buy this workout apparatus and get jacked!" I'm here to tell you that's almost entirely false. I've done every kind of workout in existence, from Yoga, Pilates, Power Lifting, Bodyweight, Cardio, the entire breadth of workouts. Let me detail this a little further. Of course, there are tons of different workout plans with different goals, and they all have their value. What I'm saying is that unless you are a bodybuilder or going for a specialized activity, the workout doesn't matter. What matters, is that you pick one and stick to it. Maintaining some level of activity, every day is the key. The Iron Mind requires consistency, so whether it's lifting or Yoga, you have to ritualize it. Now, I will give you the plans I've used, but by no means is that full breadth of workouts. Find what works for you, and stick to it. Look, there are a million different plans out there. Some use high repetitions lower weight, and vice versa.

Now, I said find what works for you. That doesn't mean you can walk a quarter mile a day and call it good. You have to push yourself. Get the blood thundering, and your breathing hard. This is how the Iron Mind is forged; in the crucible of battle with yourself. My ego used to dominate me, I already wanted to lift harder than anyone around me, and I worried so much about what others thought. "Will this girl like me" or "am I stronger than that guy." The reality is, I'm nowhere near as powerful as I was pre-injury, but I'm happier. I no longer care if anyone likes it, or if someone is lifting harder than I am. The only thing that matters is, am I challenging myself? Am I taking it to my limits, and surpassing yesterday? That's what matters. I'm not the biggest, fastest, or strongest, but I think I look damn good for a 40-year-old, and better than I did at 20.

I love working out in the morning, for a few reasons. One, I've just slept, so my energy levels are unaffected by anything that's gone on throughout the day. Second, starting with a workout gives a sense of accomplishment and conquest before you've even started anything else. It puts you in the right frame of mind for work, or whatever else is going on that day. Third, the endorphins put you in a better mood, so you are likely to be happier through the day. I can see the value in working out at night, after consuming calories all day, but I believe the importance of starting the day off strong can't be matched. It isn't a deal breaker by any means, but I highly recommend it.

I also love being sore. Walking around all day with sore legs, or anything else is a pleasure. People complain about it sometimes, but I love it. This is simply a reframing trick like I mentioned earlier. Instead of thinking how miserable you are because of your soreness, view it as the physical manifestation of achievement, Every step that you feel your legs burning, you are feeling the growth and satisfaction of knowing you are putting forth the best version of yourself. Sometimes, I flex whatever muscle group is sore, just to remind myself of the work I've done to put myself on the right path. Remember, as I said, virtually anything can be reframed. The little everyday negatives can almost always be flipped into something positive to build your strength and determination. Always remember to look for the reframing in little everyday things, flip the negative to a growth positive.

And what do I recommend for a workout? I'll start with what I did and what I recommend for maximum strength, then I will suggest a plan for best all-around fitness and health. The first thing you need to to do is isolate what you want to achieve overall. Add muscle? Lose fat? Get toned? Incidentally, when someone says get toned, what they mean is lose enough body fat to show some semblance of muscle.

Strength and Growth

I power lifted for close to 20 years. I was never the strongest, but I can tell you a 1300 pound composite lift (Bench Press, Deadlift, and Squat) is not bad for a guy with mediocre genetics. I always wore it like a badge of honor, that I was massive and really powerful, without being on steroids or growth hormone. I'll put it this way; when I started, I was

228lbs of pure fat, no muscle development at all. I then cut down to 175 and was pretty lean and ripped. Finally, At my apex, I was 270lbs. The moral of the story is, genetics and steroids aren't everything. You definitely can get pretty massive or cut without them.

Now, onto what I was doing to gain power and strength. I tried a lot of different plans. High reps, low weight, and vice versa. I also tried ten sets of 10 of a particular workout, forced negatives, all of it. Here's what I advocate for those trying to put on muscle:

1. 4 Sets of escalating weight.
2. 1st set - 20+ repetitions as a warmup
3. 2nd set - 12 repetitions max out.
4. 3rd set - 8 repetitions max out.
5. Final set - No less than 5 reps, unless you are power lifting.

Example workout split assuming five days in the gym:
1. Shoulders and Biceps
2. Legs and Abs
3. Day off
4. Chest and Triceps
5. Shoulders
6. Day off
7. Arms (Or whatever body part needs more work)

Now, at one point I was doing six heavy lifting days a week. The only way that's usually possible is if you're young, or on steroids. To fuel that sort of schedule, you have to eat like a machine and keep up the calories. I will cover more of this in the diet chapter, as you can kill yourself in the gym, but if your diet isn't right, then you won't see as exceptional results. Remember this: The gym is only an hour or so a few times a week. It is far more challenging to stay on point the other 23 hours of the day.

So what actual exercises do I recommend? There is no getting around it; the big 3 are king. Deadlift, Bench Press, and Squat in that order. Now, I prefer dumbbell presses to barbell bench presses, but whichever works for you. I would, for literally any workout type, prioritize deadlifts above all else. In my estimation, the deadlift is the king of all exercises. If a genie came out of a bottle and cursed you only to be able to do one exercise for the rest of your life, this is the one I would pick. This is my love letter to the deadlift, the most primal and king of all exercises.

1. It's primal. The weight just sits on the ground. All you have to do is pick it up.
2. You can do heavier weights on deadlifts than any other.
3. It works the entire body at a level no other exercise can. Legs, back, arms and core, all get fired and pumped at a level that can't be matched.
4. With the greatest weight, comes the greatest feeling of conquest and achievement.

This is going to sound dumb to some, but the day I deadlifted 500 pounds is one of the greatest days of my life. Nothing, not a girl, not any work achievement or paycheck has ever matched the feeling I got from that. When you pick up a weight that 99% of the population of the planet can't, it is an indescribable feeling. How many people that ever lived on this planet can do that? Not many from a percentage standpoint. Feeling the bar bend and the power course through your veins as you struggle with the most primal move of all, and overcoming it is life-defining. For some, 500 lbs isn't a lot; maybe even to some reading this. It's a lot for me though, and I worked for years to do it. This is part of the reason nothing bothers my ego anymore. I gave everything I had, and now I have nothing to prove to anyone. I don't lift like that anymore, as I've had several injuries from overdoing it, which I will discuss later.

What then do I recommend for someone who doesn't want to power lift or Max out weights?

The answer is everything.

That's right, after 20 years of lifting and being 40 years old now, I advocate a full, and complete fitness profile taking from all disciplines. I have combined Yoga, Weights, and cardio into one full fitness profile. The idea is to have no weakness, and cover everything. I believe this sort of program is ideal for those that want an exceptional all-around fitness profile. Something like this will give you strength, flexibility, endurance, and great aesthetics. It can also be one even if you have injuries, as I do. For example, here's a week long schedule:

1. Full Body Circuit of Weights with a cardio finisher.
2. 30 Minute Yoga routine, and at least 15,000 steps.
3. Arms, Shoulders, Chest.
4. Day off - 15,000 Steps.

5. Yoga and Cardio.
6. Full Body Circuit of weights with a cardio finisher.
7. Day off - 15,000 steps

Equipment

Never let anyone tell you equipment doesn't work or is for weenies. All professionals use things like lifting straps, knee wraps, and belts at some level. I know you get the hardcore gym bros acting like they are too good for equipment, and I'm here to tell you that is total bullshit. I understand that you don't necessarily need them when you are just starting out, but once you become a more advanced lifter handling higher weights, you'd be foolish not to use them. Do not let anyone else's fake machismo dictate what you use and what you lift. Remember, if you get injured, you may very well never lift again. Accordingly, use wraps, belts, or straps to introduce more stability into your routine. If you don't believe me, just go to YouTube and watch arguably the greatest bodybuilder of all time, Ronnie Coleman, squat 800 pounds. Or professional powerlifter Eric Lilliebridge do 1045 lbs. These are the top tier of the top tier, and they use strap, belts, shirts, the whole deal. Do not let your ego get you into trouble. Use the damn equipment.

Let's take a look at the best exercise for every body part. These are on this list not only through my own experience but from several personal trainers. I'm not going to describe them as there are plenty of Youtube videos you can watch to get the idea.

Back:

1. Pull-ups
2. Chinups
3. One Arm Dumbbell Rows
4. Deadlifts
5. Pulldowns
6. T-Bar Rows

Shoulders
1. Seated Dumbbell Press
2. Delt raises to the Front, Side, and Rear
3. Farmer's Walks (Also great for Back and Legs)
4. Upright Rows (Both cable and barbell)
5. Shrugs
6. Incline Press (Smith Machine)

Chest
1. Pushups
2. Dips (There's a press down machine that I love as well)
3. Dumbbell Presses (Flat, Decline, Incline)
4. Cable Crossover

Triceps
1. Dips
2. Cable Pressdown
3. Rope Extensions (overhead, standard, reverse)
4. Overhead Dumbbell Extensions

Biceps and Forearms
1. Supinating Curls
2. Hammer Curls
3. Preacher Curls

4. Reeves Incline Curls
5. 21s Bar Curls

Legs
1. Squats (Many variants, several great ones)
2. Leg Press
3. Stiff Leg Deadlift
4. Leg Curls
5. Calf Raises (Machine, Seated, Leg Press Machine)
6. Leg Extensions

Abs
1. Plank Variants
2. Leg Raises
3. Situps
4. Crunches

Remember, unless you are a bodybuilder or powerlifter the important thing is to do the work. Any workout you pick will yield results if you stick with it; then, if you want to go to the next level, get a specifically tailored program. Let me say one more thing, there are no excuses. I hear people say constantly, "I don't have time for a workout."

Yes you do.

I know people that are busier than you are that make it happen. Multiple kids, multiple jobs, the whole thing. You need to get better at time management. If you've been making those excuses, then you aren't in the right frame of mind. If I offered you a million dollars to workout for six months, I guarantee you'd find a way to make it happen. Recalibrate your priorities and understand that this is your life, and you only get one, so it better be good. I don't care if you're busy, or it's cold or rainy out, or you have the sniffles, get your ass in the gym.

Also, remember you can kill yourself in the gym with minimal results if the diet isn't right. That's where we are going next.

Chapter XXXIX

The Iron Diet

Now comes one of the more difficult parts, so I saved it for nearly the end. It's hard to be disciplined enough to go to the gym for an hour a few times a week, it's even harder to be disciplined the other 23 hours or so a day. You can murder yourself in the gym, and still not feel or look as good as you can without the right diet. I've known guys who could run an hour and a half on the treadmill, and still not have a magnificent physique. For myself, I didn't start making enormous improvements in my physique until I understood the importance of the diet, even more so than working out. First though, let me just say I don't particularly like the term "Diet." That label implies it's a short-term thing. I'll use it for shorthand, but understand that I always mean food lifestyle. Remember earlier when I talked about systems vs. goals? We want a food system that keeps us healthy, not one that we stop once we hit a target weight.

Key: Physique is 75% Diet, 25% Workouts.

Here's my physique theory: It is possible to have the Iron Mind without a great physique, but it helps a lot if you do. Now, when I say "great physique" I'm not talking about super ripped fitness models. I'm just talking a standard, decent looking, healthy BMI physique. Don't get caught up in body dysmorphia trying to get the perfect look, unless you are a bodybuilder or fitness model. Every once in awhile you see a grossly obese person claiming they are totally satisfied with being overweight. They are lying to themselves, and they think if they do it long enough it will be true. Do not get caught up in this sort of "body positive" movement. If there were a button to push that would instantly give them an amazingly aesthetic physique, every one of them would push it. They just don't want to do the work necessary to get it, so they try to lie to themselves about how happy they are.

Remember, the goal here is to feel great, both mentally and physically. The diet is beyond critical to both. It's easy to artificially and temporarily feel good through eating a pizza or ice cream, as those stimulate chemicals in our brain that makes us feel good. I wrote earlier about how our food impacts our mental state, but the harder thing is to feel good regularly. Maintaining personal energy and a positive attitude throughout the day can be tough, especially on a restricted diet. Now, I will tell you another secret:

Key: Almost all diets work. Pick the one you can stick with long term.

I have done virtually all diets to some level of success. I've done Keto and Atkins, Carb Cycling, High Fat/Low Fat; you name it. I can tell you this, they all work if you stick to them. So this becomes the key, finding one you can stick to for an indefinite period. The most miserable I've ever been on a diet was Atkins and other low carb diets, but I know people that love them. I've done them long term, and I can tell you they definitely work, and moreover, they produce quick results because of how quickly they get rid of water weight. However, I've never felt worse. The low carbs kill my energy levels and strength in the gym, for at least a week until your body adapts. Accordingly, I don't do those anymore; but I will say, they are hard to beat if you just want to drop weight quickly. Eliminating carbs also will cause you to lose water weight. This is why fighters cut carbs to make weight before a fight. We all hold subcutaneous water beneath our skin, and cutting carbs reduces the amount of water we retain, thus making us look more ripped.

I say again: the best diet is the one you can stick to long term. I moved away from Atkins and Low Carb because even though I have the will, I prefer to have more energy and feel better during the day and doing workouts. I now prefer a 40/40/20 program. That is 40% Protein, 40% Quality Carbs, 20% Fat. I find that this breakdown works best for me, allowing enough energy, while still keeping the body fat in check. The key to staying faithful to a diet is being disciplined in the grocery store. That's one thing I've always been good at managing. If you can remain faithful in the store, that goes a long way. I can't count how many times I wanted something unhealthy, but didn't feel like leaving the house to get something. The ability to stay strong in the grocery store is critical, so never shop hungry if at all possible.

Key: There can be a massive nutritional difference in the same product type.

Here's an example. I love BBQ sauce, and I use it at least 3-4 times a week. I had been using standard Sweet Baby Rays, or something similar. Then I discovered Stubbs. Stubbs is the best tasting BBQ sauce I've ever had, but here's the key: It has almost a third of the calories and sugar. The taste is entirely due to flavor, not sugar. This is an example of a small change that you can make to not only improve the taste but the caloric intake as well. Remember that there is a lot of great tasting food out there, you just have to make smart decisions about which products to add to your diet.

Here's another myth of weight loss: Diet soda is bad. I've read article after article on this because I drink three diet sodas a day. At first, I started hearing Aspartame was dangerous for you, but that claim is unsubstantiated[1]. So the argument morphed into "Diet soda is bad because it's sweet, thus it will make you want other sweets." I find this ridiculous. I love Diet Dr. Pepper, and I view it as almost a treat. Also, it's a treat with ZERO calories. That cannot be beaten. If I can get a zero calorie treat, I'm going to use it all day. The most ripped I ever was, I was drinking Diet soda consistently. Now, you also want to include plenty of water. This is easy for me because I'm a compulsive ice eater. I eat tons of ice, in addition to my regular water intake. The point is, Diet soda is fantastic, and I'd recommend drinking nearly as much as you want. Anytime I can use something that tastes good and has zero calories, I'm all over it.

Key: Cheat on a schedule, and abuse zero calorie items.

Now here comes another tricky part: Cheating. Do I cheat on my diets? Absolutely. Let me tell you something; my cheat meals would give some a heart attack just thinking about eating them. I'm talking large pizzas with a dessert item as well. I go ballistic when I cheat, I once spent 20 dollars at Taco Bell, and that is incredibly difficult. I schedule my cheat

---

[1] https://www.healthline.com/health/aspartame-side-effects#natural-alternatives

meals, so if I'm dieting, then it's one every two weeks. If I'm just eating clean, which is normal, then I have one cheat meal every week. I'll tell you, you will never taste anything as good as your preferred cheat food after dieting hard for two weeks. Use it as a reward. It serves several purposes:

1. It gives you something to look forward to.
2. It will taste better than anything you've had in your life.
3. It's a "shock to the system" as your body adapts.
4. It's a reward for a job well done

I can't prove this scientifically, more an observed theory, but I do believe there is an element of adaptation to the human body. If we do the same workouts and eat the same things, the body tends to adapt to those habits. That's why I advocate changing up exercises periodically and having an enormous cheat meal once in awhile. Now, don't get caught in the trap of justifying ones you haven't earned. Just because you worked out one day isn't a license to go to Hardees and eat a bacon, egg, and cheese biscuit. Manage your cheats, and keep them on schedule.

Key: All that matters for weight loss: Burn more calories than you take in.

This is the cardinal rule. A lot of people want to overcomplicate this, but at the end of the day, if you eat fewer calories than you burn, you will lose weight. You could theoretically eat Twinkies all day, and if you were in a calorie deficit, you'd still lose weight. As a matter of fact, there is actually a story of a professor that did exactly that. There's a whole category of people out there now that believe that being fat is genetic. Now, it is possible to have an endomorphic physique, which means it is easier for your body to store fat and has higher insulin sensitivity, but at the end of the day, calories in and out are what matters. I have an endomorphic physique, and I've managed to get both massive and super lean at different times. It's challenging, but it's doable. So what are the body types?

1. Ectomorph: Predisposed to be a leaner, thinner body. (Sprinters)
2. Endomorph: Slightly bigger, but more disposed to carry fat.
3. Mesomorph: Predisposed to carry a broader, more muscular frame. (NFL Players)

So, what about those Ectomorphs, the ones that want to gain muscle or weight, but seem to stay skinny? I have the answer: You have to out-eat your metabolism. I hear this all the time from skinny guys, "I eat constantly and never gain weight." Then you don't eat enough; it's that simple. Some people have to eat 7000 calories a day to gain weight. That is very difficult to do. I once did 4500 a day to bulk up, and even that was rough. It felt like I was eating constantly, and was always full. I sure gained weight though, I went from 175 to 270, and it was brutal. The point is, for those ectomorphs that can't seem to gain weight, you have to eat more. At one point I was drinking a 1000 calorie shake to add calories. What's difficult, is eating that much without adding a bunch of fat. It's not that hard to hit 4000 calories if you eat an entire pizza every day. Doing it clean is rough, but if you want a physique like Hugh Jackman in Wolverine, that's what's necessary. He committed chicken genocide over those movies, eating a massive amount of chicken and clean calories, while training like a madman.

Key: For hard gainers, out eat your metabolism.

So how do I find out how much I need to eat? BMI caloric calculators can get in range, but to find out you have to test it on yourself. For me, I've done it so long that I can tell within a bowl of cereal if I'm over or not. It helps to measure and count calories, and weigh yourself every day. It's a pain at first, because you have to learn what your BMR is, and the best way to do it is counting calories and portions. After a little bit of time and experience, you'll be able to eyeball it far more efficiently. In the beginning, though, I recommend logging everything, whether its weights or diet. Nowadays, it's much easier to track things with smartphones. No more lugging around a notebook full of numbers to track. Back in the 90s and early 2000s, I would have murdered someone to have access to the technology we have now. You can even just scan items at the store and at restaurants to get a caloric measurement. The tools are there to make this much more comfortable than it used to be, so use them.

Key: Log and measure everything, until you can eyeball it.

So what foods and supplements do I recommend? First, let's get the Iron Foods on the table. The Iron Foods are the ones that you could eat at every meal, and you'd be better off for life. The ones that have the highest concentration of nutrients and minimal if any sugar.

1. Chicken Breast
2. Salmon
3. Oatmeal
4. Egg Whites
5. Vegetables

6. Nuts
7. Rice

Those are the Iron Foods. Some combination of those is going to be good. I would recommend a protein source, carb source, and a vegetable at every meal. Along with a diet soda, some combination of those items have been mainstays in my diets for over 20 years. Now, learn to be smart. Any one part will get old after awhile, so learn to change them up. There are a thousand different recipes for each one of those items, and combined present a nearly infinite array of meals.

So here's the rule we want: One Protein, Fat, Fruit and vegetable, and Carb source with every meal. For me dinner lines up like this:
1. Steak, Chicken, or Salmon.
2. A small handful of Almonds, Pecans, and Cashews.
3. A small serving of Broccoli and Carrots.
4. A small scoop of Brown Rice.

Sounds boring, doesn't it? I like the ritual. It helps me stay in line, and I can make massive amounts of that stuff once and eat it all week. The other element is that if I remain rock solid on a diet, I can justify a mega cheat meal every so often. I talked about the reasoning for cheating above, and let me tell you when I say cheat, I mean cheat big. For me, it's an entire Dominos Pan Pizza, and maybe even a side of their Cinnamon Twists. I don't play around; once I've earned that cheat, I'm going to use it, big time. Again though, you don't get to do this without being rock solid the rest of the time. Lately, it's been once every two weeks, but when I'm not actively cutting weight, it's a week or less. For me, the reality is that if there are over 21 meals in a week, and 19 or 20 of them are clean, then I'm good. I'm not a big fan of eliminating certain foods forever, I've always thought that was foolish.

Treat yourself, but only if you paid the price. Here is the final trick to the diet: Get addicted to the way eating clean makes you feel. Once you get in even semi-decent shape, and eat clean regularly, you will feel appreciably better. I have gotten to the point where I don't WANT to eat junk constantly, and that takes time and effort. I'm addicted to feeling great, having high energy, and looking awesome. A lot of that is mind frame, as we've talked about, but a lot of it takes work and diet.

Now that we've talked workout and diet, lets move to recovery.

Chapter XXXVIII

The Magic of Massage

In this chapter, I'm here to tell you about the absolute magic of massage. More specifically Trigger point massage. For years and years, I had problems with my back. Somehow it always seemed like I injured myself working out, but also at mundane times. I'd wake up with a crick in my neck, or a tight back. Sometimes I'd pull something so badly I couldn't even hold my head straight. This went on for over a decade. Me continually battling with my various injuries and muscle pulls trying to stay in the gym and keep working out. So one day with my back pulled for the umpteenth time, I went to a masseuse. They pushed around all over my back eventually touched a spot that exploded with pain. It was unbelievable how bad it hurt, and they hadn't even pushed hard at all. They went all over my back, shoulders, and even sides, and every so often a particular spot would just put me in agonizing pain.

This is where I learned what "trigger points" are. They are spots where the muscle has knotted up due to over contraction. When I get one, a lot of times I can physically feel the knot, and just touching it causes an explosion of pain. So, after discovering the existence of my problem I'd had all these years, I set about trying to fix it. Apparently, the key to a trigger point is rubbing with a fair amount of pressure all over the knot to get it to loosen up. Now, I don't know about you, but I can't afford a masseuse every four days to massage all the knots out of my body, so I had to learn how to do it myself. First thing I'd do is heat up the area with a heating pad to allow for better circulation. Once I had done that for about 20 minutes or so, I'd take a ball (Tennis ball or equivalent) and lean up against the wall and use the ball to rub out the knots. I should tell you this:

Be ready for unbelievable pain.

This takes an iron will to really get through. It will hurt so bad you will be nearly in tears, but you have to keep the pressure on. You don't even have to necessarily roll the ball over the affected area, just have it on the affected area with pressure from the leaning. Do this on affected areas in your back, neck, and under your arms, and I promise you it will change the game 100% if you've been having these types of problems. Now keep in mind, warming up especially once you get older, is absolutely critical. When I was 25, I was borderline invincible. I could run around the gym and sling heavy weights with little to no warm up. Those days are over now. So I have to really get loose before touching any kind of weights, or its a quick path to injury now.

Do not take anything for granted. I used to think a trip to the gym was just another thing I did until it got taken away by injury. Now I take every exercise seriously and treasure every workout. I still get injured once in awhile, but overall I do much better than I used to. The moral of the story is, take care of your body. Do the extra few minutes of warming up or massaging knots. It will pay dividends in the long run, I assure you. Now I'm going to give a piece of advice that I have failed at myself for years. I'm better at it now, but I failed at this for years, and it cost me big:

Take time off when you need to.

For a while, when I was in my gym and lifting prime, I just couldn't bear to be out of the gym. Injured or sick, it didn't matter. I had to go. And I've paid the price. Both of my elbows had to be reconnected because I just couldn't bear to wait for things to heal. I overworked an already injured body because I was so desperate to keep my muscle, and in the end, lost even more because of it. I know it's hard. Once you get in that habit of conquering at the gym, it becomes addictive, and you can't stand to miss a day. I've been there. Monitor your body, you only have one, and you don't want to screw it up permanently. If you are an elite athlete, and you need the extra day off for recovery, take it. Get plenty of sleep as well, and build up your return in your mind. I didn't take a lot of days off, but when I did, I'd build my return up in my mind as the Return of the King or something. Two days in advance or so, start thinking about how insane that next workout is going to be. Set it up and visualize the domination in your mind for the next few days, and by the time that workout comes around, you will be primed for devastation.

Take care of your body, give it what it needs, then crush it.

Chapter XL

Supplements: A Cautionary Tale

Understand one thing: the old time bodybuilders, guys who had godlike physiques, didn't need supplements. Steve Reeves was born in 1926, and had a physique like a greek god. He didn't need pre-workout formulas, or any crazy concoctions. He had drive, desire, and that's all he needed to craft a physique that surely resides in the pantheon of Mount Olympus. Even the old school bodybuilders like Franco Columbo, Frank Zane, and Arnold didn't need to blow huge sums of cash on supplements. I decided to add this section because in retrospect over my life, I honestly can't think of any one thing I've wasted more money on than supplements. I'm doing this section so I can lay out the ones I stick with, and what has and hasn't worked. The first thing to understand about supplements is the sheer amount of confirmation bias involved. If you expect a supplement to do something magical, there's a good chance you will go out of your way to make it happen, regardless of the actual effect of the supplement itself. This is why the reframing steps I talked about earlier are so necessary. You can convince yourself something is true. So, when you go buy a new supplement, you are primed to see results. The shredded guys in the ad, coupled with some vague new ingredient you've never heard of, and your readiness to buy into the confirmation bias will have you ready to rock by the start of your first workout. On this new magic supplement, you've convinced yourself that you are King Kong in the gym, only to have that magic wear off eventually once your confirmation bias ends. I've bought into this line of events more times than I care to admit.

So after all these years of powerlifting and bodybuilding, what are the mandatory supplements that I would recommend, that have held their own way past any confirmation bias fueled arguments?

Caffeine: Unquestioned. If you are looking for energy, here it is. And moreover, you don't need to spend a zillion dollars on some pre-workout craziness; you can get energy in a caplet for next to nothing. Also, I'm not a coffee fan, but hey knock yourself out on the coffee, just don't go crazy with the creme and sugar. It's not a dessert. This is why a lot of people swear by black coffee pre-workout. It raises core temperature and pumps the caffeine, so it can power serious workouts.

Creatine: Creatine works by allowing your body to hold more water, thus making you appear to be bigger than what you actually are. For some, this will result in bloating and water retention that is just fake weight, but hey, I don't mind looking fake muscular, to be honest. And for that, it definitely works.

Protein: Obviously if one is trying to build muscle, this is pretty necessary. You aren't a horse that can get super jacked from hay and grass. They have different digestive systems that process these things differently, so they can get what they need from those things that you can't. If you are trying to build muscle, protein is a requirement. Depending on how you structure your diet, I usually go with approximately 1 gram to 1.25 grams per pound of bodyweight a day. Those on low carb diets can go even higher.

Citrulline Malate: This is one of the new-fangled supplements I heard about years ago that seemed promising, and turned out after many years of studies to be the real deal. Increasing Nitric Oxide production to look better and decreasing lactic acid for more stamina is absolutely a winner. Past the basics of vitamin, protein, creatine; this would be one of my first additions.

Basic multivitamin: You don't need anything crazy here, just something to fill in the nutritional gaps. Look, I can find multiple studies that say you don't need one, and multiples that say you should have one. This, like most supplements, is pretty controversial, but I lean in the direction of taking it. They aren't expensive, so this is one that I realize still has some confirmation bias involved, but I do it anyway.

The moral of this chapter is make sure that you can see past fake reviews, confirmation bias, and hype. The basics have been the building blocks for decades, so make sure you aren't wasting tremendous money as I have in pursuit of some mythical physique. If you want the godlike physique, it's going to take killer workouts, fantastic diet, and iron will. There is no magic bullet. The supplement industry will try to convince you every day that there's some new magical elixir that will give you the body of Hercules, so be on the lookout, and only buy into stuff that's proven over time. Remember that they are called "supplements" for a reason. They are supplementary to an actual diet and workout. None of them are going make you a demigod, so understand where the priorities should be, the workouts and proper diet.

Chapter XLI

Books are Power

I spent a lot of years reading nothing more significant than the back of a cereal box. My logic was that I was watching a lot of TV and movies and even playing games, so that was the equivalent of reading. I was a "media relativist" who thought that all of these were created equal, and consuming one over the other made little difference.

How wrong I was.

I was a voracious reader as a child. I consumed books like a vacuum. Once video games came along, I allowed them to supplant my books and didn't think twice about it. I went years without reading a single thing of substance. My vocabulary was still pretty good from all the reading I did as a child, so I used that as an excuse to not read any further. I thought hey, I feel pretty smart; I use big words periodically, so I'm doing just fine. Over the course of time, I started to feel I was lagging behind in my knowledge base. I wasn't able to think particularly profoundly about topics, with only a cursory understanding, and I assumed I had missed out on something, as I've never read many of the classics.

Once I started my new venture, I was woefully behind the knowledge curve. So I made a conscious decision to begin crushing books and make up for lost time. Since I started, I've read dozens of dozens of books from every possible range, from Marcus Aurelius to Ta-Nehisi Coates. Karl Marx to Ann

Coulter. I've set up a cycling list of types of books to read to ensure I get as much variance as possible.

1. Fiction
2. Self Improvement e.g. diet, mindset, workout
3. Classic literature
4. Philosophy/Theory/meditation
5. Personal choice
6. History
7. Fiction
8. Poetry
9. Political
10. Repeat

I've also set a goal of an hour and a half a day, at two 45 minute increments. Sometimes more. We have become a society that just rots away in front of the TV, and we don't exercise our brains like we used to in years gone by. For me, I used to tell myself I'd rather see someone execute on TV the vision from the book, rather than interpreting it myself. That's fine, because some of the filmmakers these days are incredible, coupled with the insane special effects we have now, we can put entire worlds on the screen as never before. Keep in mind though: watching it doesn't improve ancillary skills like your vocabulary, writing ability or cognition in the way reading does. You painting the picture exercises your mind in a way that games or movies never can. If you are trying to be happy in life, and are trying to get somewhere, then you have to read. Fortunately, you've already proved you can read something by buying this book and making it this far.

Do not allow this to be the last book you read for five years. Challenge yourself. Think of it this way: on the schedule, I mentioned earlier, depending on your speed of reading and comprehension, you could theoretically do 3+ books a month. Now think of this: imagine reading 3+ books on the SAME topic. By the time you are finished, you'd be at an extremely high tier of understanding of that one topic, far more than the majority of the planet. Think of how many topics you could have mastered over the last few years of not reading. You could have become a master of several areas in that span of time. Also, maybe you don't want to read about the same topic for a month. Take my list above, for instance, Using that structure you could gain a breadth of knowledge and perspective that's untouchable by the majority of people walking this earth.

The question is: How bad do you want it?

If you made it this far: I wouldn't bet against you. Now let's take a look at the most precious commodity in existence: Time.

Chapter XLII

The Time Spiral

When I was younger, I didn't care about time. I viewed it as an endless stream that I was lazily drifting down. Waste a day sleeping here, playing video games there, getting drunk, or binging a Netflix series; it really didn't matter. When you are young, and you have your entire life in front of you, especially in an age of hyper addiction and apathy, it is harder than ever to be motivated to conserve the one resource that can't ever be replenished: Time. You can't steal more of it, buy it, negotiate for it, or beg to get more of it. It wasn't until I was in my 30's that the concept of time really started to kick in for me.

The life expectancy is for a United States male is 77, which is actually ranked 32nd in the world. That means that as I sit here and type this, my life is over half done. Maybe that realization is why I am trying to wring every last drop out of life, and why you have to wake up and do the same. Setting aside the fact that you could die at any time, let's say you manage to live it all the way out, to 80 years old. What will you be thinking on your deathbed? I can assure you it won't be how awesome the hundreds of hours you poured into a particular video game were, or how fabulous Daredevil was on Netflix. It will be the sum total of the experiences you had, the friends and family, the love you gave and received, the knowledge you gained and the places you visited and the impact you had. The point of this chapter is not to get all morbid on you; it is to make you realize that you have to take time seriously, starting right now.

I've been fascinated by the future recently. More specifically, how I might live on through the ages. Publishing this book, barring any sort of Fahrenheit 451 type book burnings, means at least a small fragment of myself will live on in perpetuity, for all eternity, until the end of civilization. Even if no one buys a single copy of this book, it's entirely possible someone a thousand years from now will find it, and glean something from it. I watched an episode of the TV show Black Mirror once, that centered around resurrecting a loved one through technology. Basically, the technology parsed every single text, video, and record of that person and recreated them digitally. I realized recently that including my book and articles, I've written over 150,000 words. I've texted thousands of times and written a similar amount of email. There are quite literally hundreds of videos of me online as well. I have thousands of tweets and comments all over the internet, about every conceivable subject in which I've ever been interested. In other words, I've put enough information about myself out there, that a sufficiently advanced artificial intelligence could, with incredible accuracy and enough processing power, literally recreate me digitally.

I then thought to myself, what pieces would be missing if I were to be recreated digitally? How expansive would the knowledge base be? How big would the storage and processing power need to be to hold the sum total of all my experiences and knowledge? The answer was: not powerful enough. I want to know and have experienced so much, that even a future civilization would struggle to recreate me. To do that, I have to start taking time more seriously. I need to start wringing every last second out of each day, learn and experience as much as possible. In other words, I have to get really good at managing time. Let me stress first that doesn't mean stopping recreational activities. I still enjoy movies, music, games, and TV. I've just gotten much better at managing them, and not allow them to dominate my life. I will lay out a few time management techniques in this chapter that I use, and help you do the same to get your time in order.

First up, I will address one area that a lot of people need significant work in:

Sleep.

I view sleep as a colossal waste of time. To be honest, I wish I didn't have to do it all. Unfortunately, I need 8 hours to function correctly, especially given my workouts that drain me to a significant degree. I do not want one minute beyond that, and naps are out of the question. I know people that sleep upwards of 10 hours a day, which I can't even comprehend. When you are sleeping, you are accomplishing and doing absolutely nothing. Imagine if you slept 10 hours a day for 20 years. That is two hours a day that has vanished into the ether, which gave you nothing in return. 14,600 hours, or 608 days gone forever. What could you have done in life with more than 600 extra days? How much could you have learned, felt, experienced, or created in that time? The point of this thought experiment is to get you to understand the significance of time, and get it under control. Do not sleep more than absolutely necessary. If you are one of those people that can get away with 5 hours a night, do it. Three extra hours a day is a game breaker regarding life. The point is this: do not waste your life sleeping, but make sure you get enough. If that needs to be 8 hours, then do it, but do not go over 8.

Now let's get some productivity in line. If you sleep 8 hours a day, that means you have 16 other hours to accomplish everything you need out of life to be happy. As you read earlier, introducing dogma and ritual into your life can make a huge difference in getting your life together and putting in a place that makes you happy. Learning to focus better without distraction means your output will be higher quality. By this part of the book, you should have everything you need to maximize those 16 hours. I will, however, add a few more productivity tips.

Find a productivity method that works for you, first and foremost.

There are a ton of different methods out there, whether it be Pomodoro methods, work blocks, staggered breaks, GTD (Getting Things Done) models, Don't Break the Chain, etc. My personal favorite is Work Blocks. I like to set aside X time to obliterate everything critical in my list for the day. The point is to find one that suits you best, whether it's knocking out gigantic spreadsheets, or writing a book. Do something relaxing before to set the tone, and go in and crush it at full focus for X amount of time. Then do something relaxing again to wind down, then ramp the focus back up to 10. I will use this very chapter as an example. This chapter originates months ago when I watched a Periscope by Scott Adams where I heard him suggest the theory I outlined earlier about replicating oneself using technology. On my morning walk this morning, for some reason I was thinking about this topic and reviewing my online profile in my head. Around 2 pm, I was reading a bit of James Clavell's masterpiece, Shogun. Afterward I took another walk, which is where I think of most of my topics and ideas, and of course, the dog loves these walks. Upon returning, totally relaxed and fed, I crushed the first 1100 words. Around the 1000 word mark, I usually start to burn out and feel exhaustion. I took a break, had a pomegranate popsicle, walked a bit outside, and then watched a Scott Adams periscope again. I then sat down and wrote this paragraph. In other words, learn how you work best and exploit the high energy, high focus areas for maximum productivity.

I think about how much I've learned in the last eight months since I recommitted myself to reading and learning all I could. Then, I extrapolate that out to the previous 15 years or so that I didn't. I could have been an expert in multiple fields in that amount of time. Don't get me wrong, I have an incredible talent stack, and I'm not into regret, so I only bring that up to illustrate for you how critical the time is that you are flushing down the toilet. Whenever I hear someone say, "Oh I don't have time to do this that or the other thing," I think to myself, Yes you do. You just aren't sufficiently organized and motivated. I hope in reading this book, you have gleaned enough information to make radical changes in your life and to get everything you want out of it.

Thank you for reading, I really wish you the best, and if you have any questions feel free to contact me on social media.

Now go crush it.

The End.

Next Steps

I hope you've gotten something out of this book. I wanted to unload everything I possibly could with enough clarity and simplicity to get it all in one shot. You might be asking what you can do to move further on a particular concept I outlined, so I'm going to list a few books and even some movies that have had a major impact on me.

Anything by Scott Adams

Yes, I mean quite literally anything. Every book he's written is fantastic, and his persuasion filter really changed the game on how I view life.

Pumping Iron

Arnold in this movie is 100% pure Iron. This movie shows how to dominate and do what's necessary to win.

Pre-Suasion and Influence

Robert Cialdini is a leading cognitive scientist on the powers of persuasion and how to effect the human mind. Read these if you want to turn your life up to 11 and get what you want.

48 Laws of Power

This book is incredible. Slightly less ethics than your average self help book, and really has great examples. This one is not for the faint of heart, but is required reading, especially to learn how to watch your back.

Arnold's Complete Encyclopedia of Modern Bodybuilding

The only workout and diet book you will ever need.

Playing to Win

David Sirlin, a world champion Street Fighter player, teaches how not to be a scrub and gain a competitive advantage. This book was life changing for me. If you do anything competitive, this book is a must.

The Art of War

One of the most relevant classics in existence, with so many tools you can apply to modern life.

How to Win Friends and Influence people

Dale Carnegie teaches you how to amp up your networking game to 11. This coupled with Cialdini and Adams will give you all the persuasion technique you can handle.

Trump: The Art of the Deal

Do not underestimate Donald Trump, or this book. Most of what he does that mystifies his opponents can be found right in this book.

The Bible

I don't care if you are religious or not, there are tremendous lessons to be learned from the Bible. There's a reason it's the basis of an entire massive religion that's lived for millennia. Incredible lessons and values, regardless of religious affiliation.

APPENDIX A: IRON BANDS

Iron Band I: Pantera

Pantera was the ultimate game changer for me. I doubt any artist will ever be as significant to me. All the music I listened to growing up was largely fairly slow. A lot of it was depressive, as it was a lot of country and adult contemporary.

Pantera was the first time I learned how powerful lyrics could be. Here was a band telling me that I could be more, that I could achieve greater. On top of the message of power, they delivered the thunder musically like I'd never heard. This band was pure power, distilled into sonic form, and driven into my brain. Ironically, the Far Beyond Driven album cover is a giant screw inside of a skull.

They were my first metal concert as well. That was the first time I'd ever been to a show, where the music thundered into my soul. I'd never felt this kind of power before, and they were telling me that I could be powerful as well. They didn't make a lot of albums, but the ones they did were pure power.

Choice Cuts:
1. Cowboys From Hell
2. A New Level
3. Fucking Hostile
4. Becoming
5. Living Through Me
6. Walk
7. Strength Beyond Strength
8. Cemetery Gates
9. This Love

10. War Nerve

Iron Band II: Danzig

Glenn Danzig is my personal favorite artist of all time. First of all, no one else sounds like him. He is sometimes referred to as "Evil Elvis" for his completely unique vocal delivery. He also has the unique ability to be extremely dark, while still somehow keeping the listener in a positive mindframe. I've seen him live at least ten times, and even at 60 he can bring energy unlike anyone I've ever seen. In addition, he was one of the first inspirations I had to work out. In the 90s, he was absolutely ripped and exuded power and energy unlike anyone else. Even in his 60s, he's still in pretty good shape.

He has a legacy of incredible work, going back to the Misfits. My "Danzig Ultimate" playlist is more than triple the size of all my other playlists with over 60 songs that I consider top tier.

Choice Cuts:
1. Twist of Cain
2. Devil's Plaything
3. Black Mass
4. On a Wicked Night
5. Last Ride
6. The Revengeful
7. Am I Demon
8. Her Black Wings
9. How The Gods Kill
10. Mother

Iron Band III: Sabaton

Sometimes the best motivation does not rise from fantasy, but from real life. Sabaton's entire arsenal of songs is comprised of entirely real historical stories of war. I've actually learned a tremendous amount about history from these guys. After hearing a song and reading the lyrics, inevitably a trip to the internet follows shortly thereafter. So in addition to real stories of heroism, which are inherently motivating, they also have ferociously catchy hooks and head banging riffs. This becomes a near magical combination for material to really motivate you in the gym, and even on just normal days. Put the windows down in your car on a spring day, turn these guys up loud and you're in for a great day.

Choice Cuts:
1. Screaming Eagles
2. Night Witches
3. 40 to 1
4. Primo Victoria
5. Ghost Division
6. Carolus Rex
7. To Hell and Back
8. The Last Stand
9. Wolfpack
10. Panzerkampf

Iron Band IV: Powerwolf

I honestly thought these guys were a joke. They are a German Power Metal theme band, meaning all of their music is based around one theme: Werewolf Priests. That's right, these guys basically role play Werewolf Priests going to war against the unholy. It sounds and looks pretty cheesy. However, these guys, maybe more so than any other band, have figured out how to distill drug addiction into a sonic form. I've never heard a band with such addicting riffs and choruses in my life. And somehow, despite being thematically very similar song to song and album to album, they never get old. Much in the way one can be addicted to heroin and the high never gets old, Powerwolf can get me head banging and pumped every time.

I can, quite literally pick an album and put it on shuffle at the gym, at its almost guaranteed to be a good workout. In addition, they keep getting better. Their latest, Blessed and Possessed, is likely their best so far. In addition to the ridiculously catchy and head banging riffs, they are ripe for the projection techniques I mentioned earlier. Any band that puts the listener into a battlefield slaying enemies works great.

Choice Cuts:
1. We Drink Your Blood
2. Higher Than Heaven
3. Armata Strigoi
4. Sanctified with Dynamite
5. Die, Die, Crucified
6. Amen and Attack
7. Sacred and Wild

8. Army of the Night
9. Christ & Combat
10. We are the Wild

Iron Band V: Agalloch

Agalloch is quite possibly my favorite band of all time. They are very obscure, even by metal standards, and it's likely that no one reading this book has even heard of them. They are one of the most unique bands ever, they are sort of a black folk metal band, that embraces primalism, naturalism and to a degree, paganism. Their lyrics are woven tapestries, weaving around themes of nature, death, paganism, but most of all the supremacy of the natural world. I've listened to them for decades, and still can't unravel all the mysteries and depth of their lyrics. Even though they are metal, they linger in a place that stands beyond genre, that ascends past mere classification.

They no longer exist, having broken up some time ago, but their legacy stands. The few albums they made are unparalleled in quality, and none are short of the masterpiece description. I would be challenged to even pick a favorite album, or even song. They, unlike any other band, must be experienced in a vacuum of the intended album. I refuse to even make a greatest hits playlist, as I usually do. The albums must be experienced in their entirety to appreciate. This is why they are the only band I will list without choice cuts. Each album stands alone as a monument and should be experienced that way. However, I will say that Pale Folklore and The Mantle exist as likely the two greatest albums I have ever experienced.

Iron Band VI: Slayer

Pantera was the game changer, but Slayer was the first. I'll never forget, my friend had just gotten a new subwoofer in his tiny truck. The first time I rode with him, he said "Ever heard Slayer?" And proceeded to play Angel of Death at near maximum volume. Life was never the same. That tiny truck with a massive subwoofer pounded pure power into my brain, and everything changed.

They were my first real venture into the vast landscape of metal. Simplicity and brutality describe Slayer. They have a very specific formula, and they've been around over 30 years. You read their lyrics, and they sound horrific. How could anyone glean anything positive? In the 80's they were one of the main targets of the censorship of the Parents Council.

How can a band who talks about dismembering people constantly, generate positive mental frame? Easy, you imagine you are the one doing it, not having it done to you. Picturing myself dominating scenes of warfare as I plowed through the weights in the gym, or another mile on the treadmill, always helped me feel like a conqueror. Ironically, having this ferocious mentality in the gym, keeps me very Zen outside of it. This is why learning to reframe your mind is so important. Take something that is negative, and reframe it to a positive. We will talk more about that later.

Slayer is proof that complex is not always better than simple, and they have over 30 years at the top of the game to prove it.

Choice Cuts:

1. Angel Of Death
2. Raining Blood
3. War Ensemble
4. Skeletons of Society
5. Disciple
6. Threshold
7. Bloodline
8. Here Comes the Pain
9. God Send Death
10. Blood Red

Iron Band VII: Nile

Nile are, to me, the current Heavyweight Champions Of Heavy Metal Mindframing. Ironically, this is a band that I originally HATED. I listened to them and it sounded like total gibberish, so, I actively made fun of them and laughed at at how stereotypical they were of Death Metal. However, I kept hearing their name. Their album, Annihilation of the Wicked, was garnering near universal praise, so I finally caved in and bought it. Upon opening the liner notes to read lyrics, I discovered they had insanely cool lyrics, accompanied by notes detailing the historical and mythological roots of the lyrics. So, I put it in, cranked it up, and followed along in the lyric book. It turns out, the founder of the band is actual an Egyptologist, and Lovecraft aficionado, and he writes with incredible research and knowledge.

What I discovered in Nile was immense power. This band can power me up like no other. If i need to power up for a major workout, or to be prepared to dominate at work, Nile's lyrics are typically the ones I recite to myself. I project myself into the lyrics as the ultimate conqueror, decimating all who oppose and stand in my way. Any obstacle is minuscule next to my power.

Choice Cuts:
1. Unas, Slayer of the Gods
2. User-Maat-Re
3. Cast Down the Heretic
4. Ithyphallic
5. Utterances of the Crawling Dead

6. Call to Destruction
7. In the Name of Amun
8. Black Seeds of Vengeance
9. Lashed to the Slave Stick
10. Annihilation of the Wicked

Iron Band VIII: Amon Amarth

Amon Amarth was my first introduction to Theme Metal. I've always loved Norse mythology and history, so when I realized there was an actual Viking Metal band, I was on board immediately. It helped that they looked like Vikings, and had impeccable power in their music. I've seen them live twice, and they literally drink beer out of horns on stage. Their power groove reminds me a lot of a Nordic version of Pantera, which is really a high compliment. It's amazing they haven't deviated once, and every song on every album is drenched in viking blood, and yet they never get old.

Their stories of Viking conquest and mythology have fueled thousands of workouts, and I can't prove it, but they might hold some kind of record for the most total minutes played in the gym for me. Not only are they a viking metal band, but I realized there are actually several viking metal bands, and its almost it's own subgenre. Have a look at Grand Magus as well, they are amazing too.

Choice Cuts:
1. Where Silent Gods Stand Guard
2. The Pursuit of Vikings
3. Runes to my Memory
4. Gods of War Arise
5. With Oden on Our Side
6. The Last With Pagan Blood
7. Destroyer of the Universe
8. Wrath of the Norsemen
9. Blood Eagle

10. Twilight of the Thunder God

APPENDIX B: IRON PLAYLISTS

Steve's Ultimate Metal Workout Playlist

Here is my Ultimate Metal Playlist. Not in any particular order, although I would recommend putting the super heavy stuff like Nile and Dying Fetus later and bands like Sabaton and Powerwolf earlier.

1. Captain America March - Alan Silvestri
2. Fire it Up - Black Label Society
3. Cast Down the Heretic - Nile
4. User-Maat-Re - Nile
5. In the Trenches - Dying Fetus
6. Triumph and Power - Grand Magus
7. The Will to Potency - Krisiun
8. Screaming Eagles - Sabaton
9. On Hooves of Gold - Grand Magus
10. Army of the Night - Powerwolf
11. Higher than Heaven - Powerwolf
12. Last Man Standing - Hammerfall
13. Built to Last - Hammerfall
14. The Last Stand - Sabaton
15. Freja's Choice - Grand Magus
16. We Drink Your Blood - Powerwolf
17. Great Heathen Army - Iced Earth
18. Edgecrusher - Fear Factory
19. Becoming - Pantera
20. Spectral War - Cavalera Conspiracy
21. Inflikted - Cavalera Conspiracy
22. The Pursuit of Vikings - Amon Amarth
23. Tattered Banners and Bloody Flags - Amon Amarth
24. Ov the Fire and Void - Behemoth

25. Hammer of the Gods - Danzig
26. Where Dragons Dwell - Gojira
27. Push the Venom - Kataklysm
28. Prevail - Kataklysm
29. Roots Bloody Roots - Sepultura
30. In the Name of Amun - Nile

AJ's Ultimate Hip-Hop Workout Playlist

I am not well versed in Hip-Hop, so I asked a friend who knows virtually everything there is to know to put one together. I took his and added a few of my favorites as well.

1. Ante Up - M.O.P.
2. BMF - Rick Ross
3. Hard in Da Paint - Waka Flocka Flame
4. MegaMan - Lil' Wayne
5. Hustle Hard Remix - Ace Hood
6. Ima Boss - Meek Mill
7. Let's Go - Trick Daddy
8. Never Scared - Bonecrusher
9. Show Out - Juicy J
10. Interlude - Lil' Wayne
11. BM Jr. - Lil' Wayne
12. Till I Collapse - Eminem
13. Fight Music - D12
14. Mama Said Knock You Out - LL Cool J
15. X got Give it to Ya - DMX
16. Lose Yourself - Eminem
17. BOB - OutKast
18. The Beast - Tech N9ne
19. Spaz Out - Army of the Pharaohs
20. Money, Power, Respect - The Lox
21. Bring Da Ruckus - Wu Tang Clan
22. M.a.a.d City - Kendrick Lamar
23. Shut em' Down - Onyx
24. Straight outta Compton - NWA
25. Energy - Drake
26. Ambitionz Az a Ridah - 2Pac

27. Close your Eyes - Run the Jewels
28. No Vaseline - Ice Cube
29. Dreams and Nightmares - Meek Mill
30. I'm Thuggin - DJ Khaled

Copyright © 2018 by Steven Mager
ISBN-13: 978-0-692-12949-4

All rights reserved.

No part of this book may be reproduced in any form or by any electronic or mechanical means, including information storage and retrieval systems, without written permission from the author, except for the use of brief quotations in a book review.

• This book is not intended as a substitute for the medical advice of physicians. The reader should regularly consult a physician in matters relating to his/her health and particularly with respect to any symptoms that may require diagnosis or medical attention.

Contact Information

You may contact me at the following locations:

Twitter: @StevenAMager

Email: AmericanaPrime@gmail.com

Web: AmericanaPrime.com